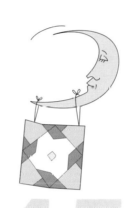

45
QUILT BLOCKS: FLOWERS

QUILT BLOCKS: FLOWERS
A New Collection of Designs

Trice Boerens

LARK
CRAFTS

A Division of Sterling Publishing Co., Inc.
New York / London

Senior Editor
Valerie Van Arsdale Shrader

Assistant Editor
Gavin R. Young

Art Director
Kathleen Holmes

Illustrator
Trice Boerens

Production
Kay Stafford

Photographer
Stewart O'Shields

Cover Designer
Pamela Norman

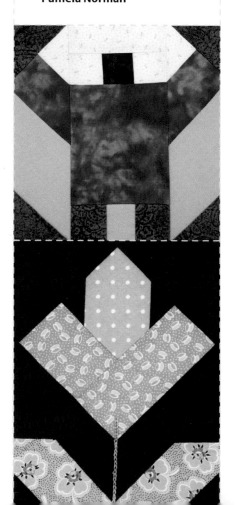

Library of Congress Cataloging-in-Publication Data

Boerens, Trice.
 45 quilt blocks : flowers : a new collection of designs / Trice Boerens.
   p. cm.
 Includes index.
 ISBN 978-1-60059-583-7 (pb-trade pbk. : alk. paper)
 1. Patchwork--Patterns. 2. Quilting--Patterns. 3. Flowers in art. I. Title. II. Title: Forty five
quilt blocks.
 TT835.B513485 2010
 746.46'041--dc22

                    2009049877

10 9 8 7 6 5 4 3 2 1

First Edition

Published by Lark Books, A Division of
Sterling Publishing Co., Inc.
387 Park Avenue South, New York, NY 10016

Text © 2010, Trice Boerens
Photography © 2010, Lark Books, A Division of Sterling Publishing Co., Inc.
Illustrations © 2010, Trice Boerens

Distributed in Canada by Sterling Publishing,
c/o Canadian Manda Group, 165 Dufferin Street
Toronto, Ontario, Canada M6K 3H6

Distributed in the United Kingdom by GMC Distribution Services,
Castle Place, 166 High Street, Lewes, East Sussex, England BN7 1XU

Distributed in Australia by Capricorn Link (Australia) Pty Ltd.,
P.O. Box 704, Windsor, NSW 2756 Australia

If you have questions or comments about this book, please contact:
Lark Books
67 Broadway
Asheville, NC 28801
828-253-0467

Manufactured in China

ISBN 13: 978-1-60059-583-7

For information about custom editions, special sales, and premium and corporate
purchases, please contact the Sterling Special Sales Department at 800-805-5489 or
specialsales@sterlingpub.com.

For information about desk and examination copies available to college and
university professors, requests must be submitted to academic@larkbooks.com.
Our complete policy can be found at www.larkbooks.com.

45 QUILT BLOCKS: FLOWERS

General Instructions

Fabric Selection

Soft fabrics that are 100-percent cotton will work best for piecing and appliqué. Use the suggested fabric colors or alter the look of your block by choosing your own palette. If you stir patterned fabric into the mix, select small-scale designs for small template pieces.

Consider both hue and value in your selections (fig. 4). The hue describes where the color falls on the color wheel; it can be pure chroma, tinted with white, or dulled with gray (fig. 1). The value describes its degree of lightness or darkness (fig. 2).

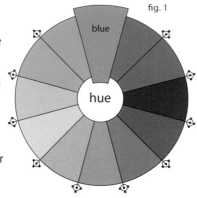

fig. 1

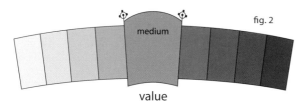

fig. 2

For subtle presentations, choose fabrics with neighboring hues and similar values (fig. 3). For blocks that snap, crackle, and pop, mix together contrasting hues and values (fig. 4).

fig. 3

fig. 4

Fabric Preparation

Make sure that your selected fabrics are colorfast, and then hand wash, dry, and press them before you begin. This will preshrink the fibers and provide you with flat working materials.

Marking Tools

You can draw fine- or medium-width lines with air-soluble marking pens. The lines will be visible for a few hours and then will disappear. Water-soluble markers are similar but the lines remain until you spritz or dab them with water. Use air or water-soluble pens to mark lines for the embroidery details. For the piecing shapes, you can use the air or water-soluble markers, a #3 pencil, or a chalk pencil.

Template Preparation

Make templates from vellum paper or from lightweight polyester film, using the diagrams in the book. Enlarge the diagram as required, place the template material on the diagram, and trace around the outside edge. Cut along the marked line. Then reverse the template and place it on the wrong side of the fabric. Align the longest side of the template with the fabric grain and hold in place. Draw around the shape with a marking pen or pencil and cut along the marked line (fig. 5). The seam allowance is represented by the interior broken lines on the diagram and is ¼" wide for the pieced shapes.

Alternatively, some quilters believe that the piecing process is more accurate if you mark the finished shape and then add the seam allowance as you cut the fabric, allowing you to sew along the marked lines. For this method, place the template material on the diagram and trace along the interior broken line. Cut out the template shape, reverse it, and place it on the wrong side of the fabric. Draw around the shape with a marking pen or pencil. Then cut around the shape ¼" from the marked line to add the seam allowance (fig. 6).

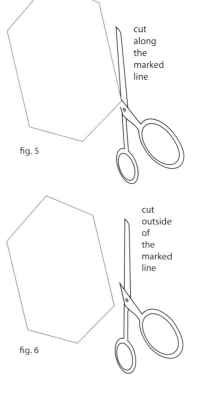

cut along the marked line

fig. 5

cut outside of the marked line

fig. 6

Machine Piecing

Pin the right sides of the pieces together and carefully feed them under the presser foot, removing the pins as you sew. Trim the threads and press each seam after sewing. At intersections, press the matching seams in opposing directions (fig. 7). Then pin the sections together with the fabric ridges pressed against each other.

When joining shapes at an angle, start and stop the seams ¼" from the fabric edges (fig. 8). So the block lies flat, the stitching lines at the ends of the seams should meet but not overlap. Individual block instructions will also include this direction when required.

If you have to adjust the seam, unpick it by pulling on the bobbin thread.

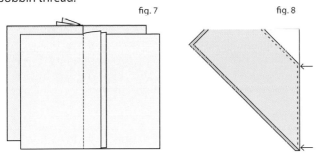

Mitered Corners

The diagonal lines of mitered corners add a jaunty angle to block designs and a crisp finish to borders. Starting and stopping ¼" from the fabric edges, sew the strips to the adjoining sides (fig. 9).

Aligning the strip edges, fold the block diagonally. Starting and stopping ¼" from the fabric edges, sew a diagonal seam at the corner (fig. 10).

Trim the excess fabric from the corner. Being careful not to cut through the seam, clip through all layers at the seam intersection (fig. 11).

Open the seam and place the block faceup on your work surface. The three seams should meet but not overlap (fig. 12).

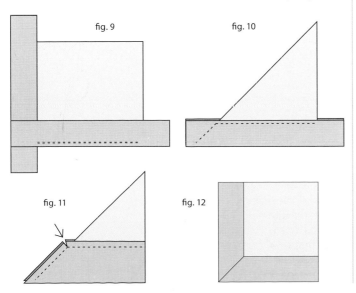

Log Cabin Border

A Log Cabin border is built with four matching strips that are offset at the corners. Begin by matching the bottom edge of the first strip to the bottom edge of the square center. Starting and stopping ¼" from the fabric edges, sew the strip to the square (fig. 13).

Sew the second strip to the adjoining side (fig. 14).

Sew the third strip to the square (fig. 15).

Starting and stopping ¼" from the fabric edges, sew the last strip to the square (fig. 16).

Realign the first and last strips and, starting and stopping ¼" from the fabric edges, sew them together at the corner (fig. 17).

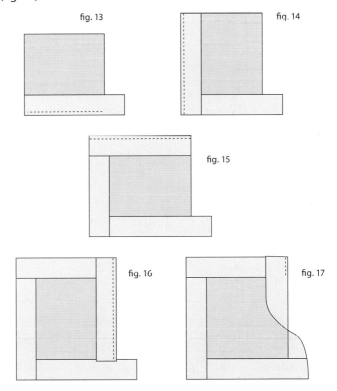

Hand Appliqué

Appliqués sit on top of the background fabric and provide easy and eye-catching embellishment. More flexible than piecing, appliqués can be straight or curved.

You will need a long, fine needle (#11 or #12 sharp), straight pins, scissors, and all-purpose sewing thread. Being careful not to cut through the fold lines, snip short perpendicular slits around and inside any curves (fig. 18), and pin the shape in place.

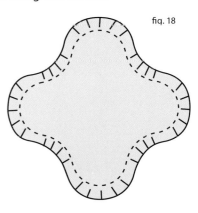

At your starting point, turn the fabric under at the broken line and finger press. For righties, work from right to left and slipstitch the shape to the background with close and even stitches. Lefties will do the opposite.

Work in small sections and use your needle to turn the edge under 1" ahead of your last stitch. When you reach a corner or a point, trim the tip before folding the edge under. This will eliminate bulk and allow the shape to lie flat. Knot the thread ends on the wrong side of the fabric to secure.

Curve Patch Piecing

A pieced block that is composed of straight lines and sharp angles can be softened with the introduction of a gentle arc. This is trickier than joining two straight sides, so baste rather than pin the pieces together. Being careful not to cut through the stitching lines, cut perpendicular slits along the curved edges of the cut shapes (fig. 19).

Match one concave shape to one convex shape. Then start in the middle and baste the shapes together along the marked lines with a running stitch. It will be necessary to realign and match the marked lines after every two or three stitches (fig. 20).

Flip the block over and work from the center to the opposite edge. Carefully machine stitch along the top of the basting stitches. Remove the basting stitches and press the pieced shape flat (fig. 21).

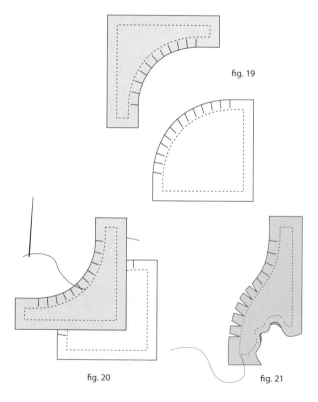

fig. 19

fig. 20

fig. 21

Embroidery

To add embroidered embellishments, use a sharp embroidery needle and two strands of floss. Knot the thread ends on the wrong side of the fabric to secure.

Running Stitch
1. Bring the needle up through the fabric and stitch evenly in an over/under pattern.

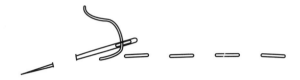

Satin Stitch
1. Bring the needle up through the fabric at A, and back down at B.

2. Make parallel stitches that fill the desired area.

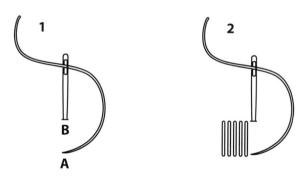

Cross Stitch
1. Bring the needle up through the fabric at A, and back down at B.

2. Then up at C and down at D.

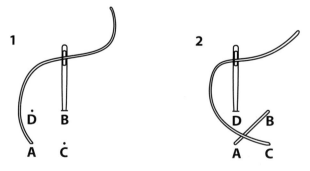

Long Stitch
1. Bring the needle up through the fabric at A, and back down at B.

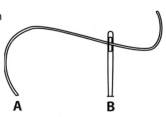

Back Stitch

1. Bring the needle up through the fabric at A, down at B, and back up at C.

2. Working right to left, insert the needle at the end of the preceding stitch and repeat.

3. Continue stitching along the marked line.

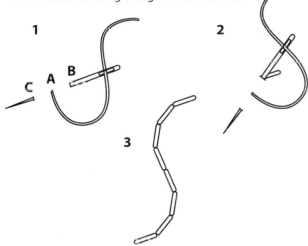

Wrapped Back Stitch

1. Refer to the Back Stitch diagrams and stitch along the marked line. Bring the needle up through the fabric at the end of the stitched line. Slide the needle under the first stitch and pull the floss through.

2. Working right to left, wrap the floss around each stitch.

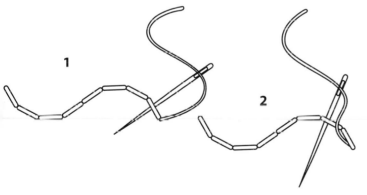

Stem Stitch

1. Bring the needle up through the fabric at A, down at B, and back up at C.

2. Working left to right, insert the needle at D and back up at the end of the preceding stitch.

3. Continue stitching along the marked line.

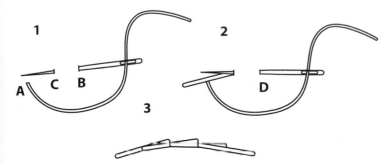

Blanket Stitch

1. Bring the needle up through the fabric at A, down at B, and back up at C.

2. Working left to right, continue along the turned edge or the marked line.

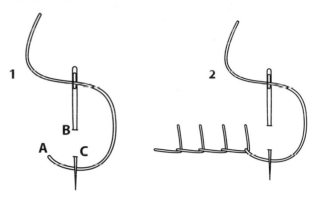

Chain Stitch

1. Bring the needle up through the fabric at A, down at B, and back up at C.

2. Working right to left, insert the needle in the center of the preceding stitch and repeat. Continue along the marked line.

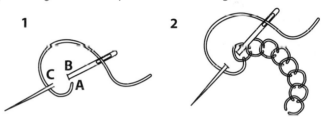

Spider Web Rose

1. Refer to the Long Stitch and make five spokes.

2. Bring the needle up at the center and in a counterclockwise direction, thread the needle over and under the spokes to make a tight coil.

3. On the outside edge of the coil, insert the needle from the front to the back and knot to secure.

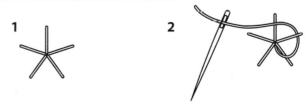

French Knot

1. Bring the needle up through the fabric, and wrap the floss around its center. Enlarge the size of the knot by wrapping the needle twice.

2. Push the needle through the fabric close to the point it emerged and pull it to the back.

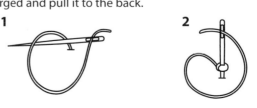

WATER LILY

Block sizes

6½" square or 8" square

Templates on page 72; enlarge 200%

Fabrics and Materials

Yellow print, white print, green print, and light blue solid

Coordinating thread

Cut the Pieces

1. From the yellow print, cut four pieces from Template A.

2. From the white print, cut four pieces from Template B.

3. From the green print, cut four pieces each from Templates C and D. Reverse Template D and cut four additional pieces.

4. From the light blue solid, cut four pieces each from Templates E and F.

Assemble the Block

1. Sew one A triangle to one B shape. Repeat to make a total of four A/B shapes. (Figure 1)

2. Sew the pieced shapes together. (Figure 2)

3. Sew the C triangles to the corners of the pieced shape to create a square. (Figure 3)

4. Sew the D shapes to the outsides of the E triangle. Repeat to make a total of four pieced strips. (Figure 4)

5. Sew two pieced strips to the square center. (Figure 5)

6. Sew the F squares to the ends of the remaining pieced strips. (Figure 6)

7. Sew the pieced strips to the square center to complete the block. (Figure 7)

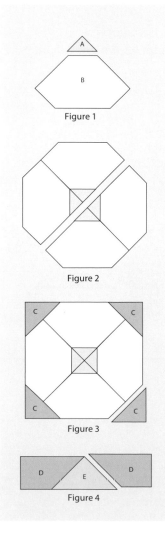

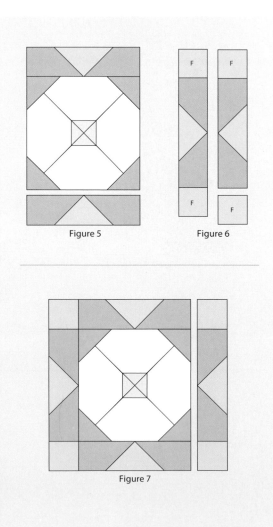

Block sizes

7" square or 8$\frac{1}{2}$" square

Templates on page 72; enlarge 200%

Fabrics and Materials

Yellow print, orange pin dot, purple print, and white solid

Coordinating thread

Cut the Pieces

1. From the yellow print, cut two pieces from Template A.

2. From the orange pin dot, cut two pieces from Template A.

3. From the purple print, cut four pieces from Template B.

4. From the white solid, cut four pieces each from Templates C and D.

Assemble the Block

1. Sew the A triangles together. (Figure 1)

2. Sew one B shape to one C shape. (Figure 2)

3. Repeat step 2 to make a total of four pieced shapes.

4. Sew two pieced shapes to the square center. (Figure 3)

5. Sew two D triangles to one pieced shape created in step 3. Repeat to make a second pieced shape. (Figure 4)

6. Sew the pieced shapes to the square center to complete the block. (Figure 5)

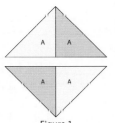

Figure 1

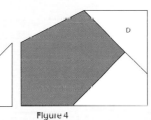

Figure 4

Figure 2

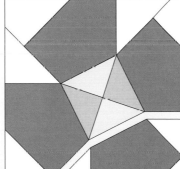

Figure 5

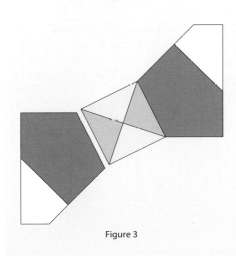

Figure 3

WILD GINGER

Block sizes

7¼" square or 8½" square

Templates on page 73; enlarge 200%

Fabrics and Materials

Purple mottle, yellow print, red mottle, green solid, and dark green print

Coordinating thread

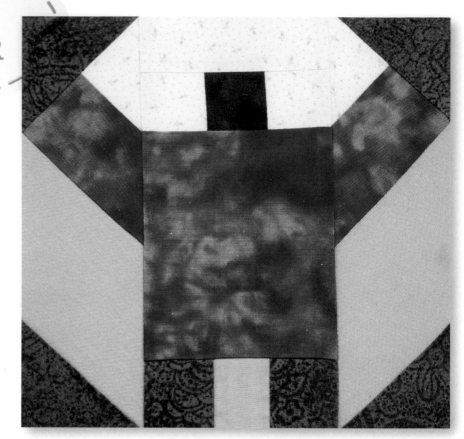

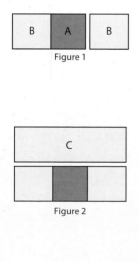

Figure 1

Figure 2

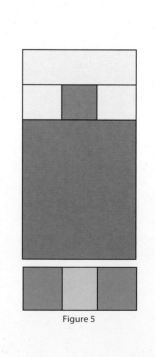

Figure 3

Figure 4

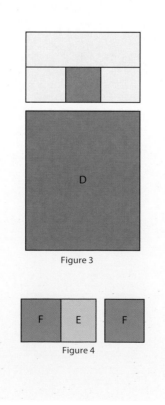

Figure 5

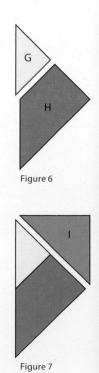

Figure 6

Figure 7

Cut the Pieces

1. From the purple mottle, cut one piece from Template A.

2. From the yellow print, cut two pieces from Template B, one piece from Template C, and two pieces from Template G.

3. From the red mottle, cut one piece each from Templates D and H. Reverse Template H and cut one additional piece.

4. From the green solid, cut one piece each from Templates E and J. Reverse Template J and cut one additional piece.

5. From the dark green print, cut two pieces from Template F and cut four pieces from Template I.

Assemble the Block

1. Sew the B rectangles to the A square to make a pieced strip. (Figure 1)

2. Sew the C rectangle to the top of the pieced strip. (Figure 2)

3. Sew the pieced rectangle to the top of the D rectangle. (Figure 3)

4. Sew the F rectangles to the E rectangle to make another pieced strip. (Figure 4)

5. Sew the new pieced strip to the bottom of the pieced rectangle. (Figure 5)

6. Sew one G triangle to one H shape, creating a larger pieced triangle. (Figure 6)

7. Sew one I triangle to one pieced triangle. (Figure 7)

8. Sew one J shape to the bottom of the pieced shape. (Figure 8)

9. Sew one I triangle to the bottom of the pieced shape, creating a long rectangular strip. (Figure 9)

10. Repeat steps 6 through 9 to make an additional pieced strip, using the pieces cut when you reversed the templates.

11. Sew the strips to the square center to complete the block. (Figure 10)

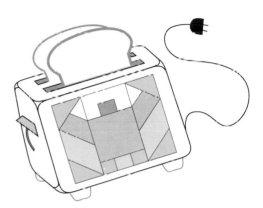

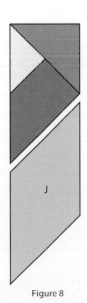

Figure 8

Figure 9

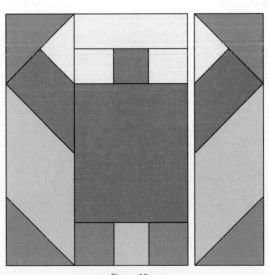

Figure 10

SUMMER BOUQUET

Block sizes

6½" square or 8" square

Templates on page 74; enlarge 200%

Fabrics and Materials

Pink print, lime print, teal print, light pink solid, and cream mottle

Coordinating thread

Figure 1

Figure 2

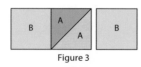

Figure 3

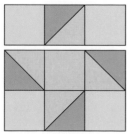

Figure 4

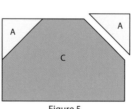

Figure 5

Figure 6

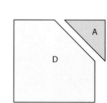

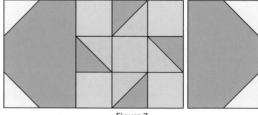

Figure 7

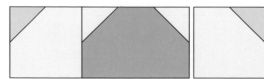

Figure 8

Cut the Pieces

1. From the pink print, cut four pieces from Template A and one piece from Template B.

2. From the lime print, cut four pieces each from Templates A and B.

3. From the teal print, cut four pieces each from Templates A and C.

4. From the light pink solid, cut eight pieces from Template A and four pieces from Template D.

5. From the cream mottle: for a 6½" block, cut four strips, each 1" x 6¾"; for an 8" block, cut four strips, each 1" x 8".

Assemble the Block

1. Sew one teal A triangle to one pink print A triangle. Repeat to make a total of four pieced squares. (Figure 1)

2. Sew two pieced squares to one pink print B square. (Figure 2)

3. Sew two lime B squares to one pieced square. Repeat to make a second pieced strip. (Figure 3)

4. Sew the strips together to create the central square. (Figure 4)

5. Sew two light pink A triangles to one C shape. Repeat to make a total of four pieced rectangles. (Figure 5)

6. Sew one lime A triangle to one D shape. Repeat to make a total of four pieced squares. (Figure 6)

7. Sew two pieced rectangles created in step 5 to the square center. (Figure 7)

8. Sew two pieced squares created in step 6 to one pieced rectangle created in step 5. Repeat to make a second pieced strip. (Figure 8)

9. Sew the strips to the square center. (Figure 9)

10. Refer to the General Instructions for the Log Cabin Border (page 7), and sew the cream mottle strips to the large square to complete the block. (Figure 10)

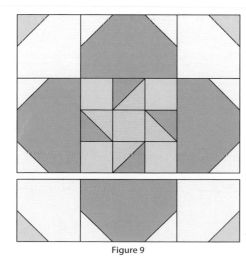

Figure 9

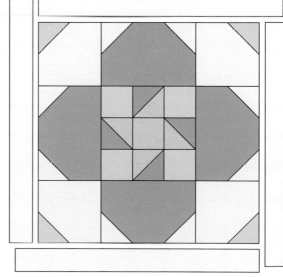

Figure 10

5 SUNRISE DAYLILY

Block sizes

7" square or 8½" square

Templates on page 74; enlarge 200%

Fabrics and Materials

White print, melon solid, brown solid, pink floral, and yellow solid

Coordinating thread

Green embroidery floss

Cut the Pieces

1. From the white print, cut one piece from Template A, two pieces from Template B, two pieces from Template D, and one piece from Template F. Reverse Template F and cut one additional piece.

2. From the melon solid, cut two pieces from Template A.

3. From the brown solid, cut one piece from Template A.

4. From the pink floral, cut two pieces from Template C and one piece from Template E.

5. From the yellow solid, cut four pieces from Template G.

Assemble the Block

1. Sew the A squares together. (Figure 1)

2. Sew one B triangle to one C shape. Sew one D rectangle to the pieced square. Repeat using the pieces cut when you reversed the template. (Figure 2)

3. Sew the E shape to one F shape. (Figure 3)

4. Trim the overlapping corner. (Figure 4)

5. Sew the remaining F shape to the pieced shape. (Figure 5)

6. Sew the pieced sections together to create the central square. (Figure 6)

7. Sew the G triangles to the square center to complete the block. (Figure 7)

8. Refer to the General Instructions for Embroidery (page 8), and use a satin stitch to make the stem. (Figure 8)

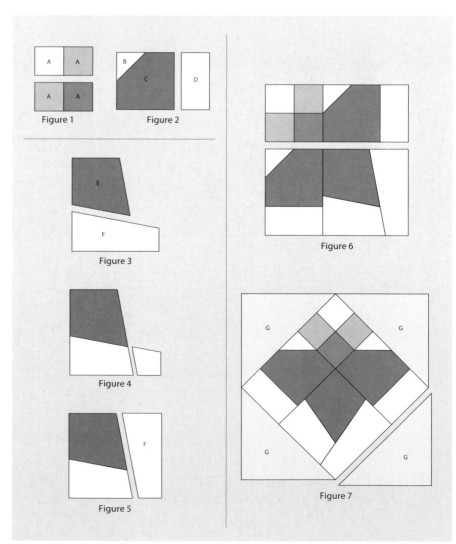

Figure 1

Figure 2

Figure 3

Figure 4

Figure 5

Figure 6

Figure 7

Block sizes

6½" square or 8" square

Templates on page 75; enlarge 200%

Fabrics and Materials

White solid, orange pin dot, burgundy solid, peach solid, and gold solid

Coordinating thread

Pink embroidery floss

Cut the Pieces

1. From the orange pin dot, cut four pieces from Template A.

2. From the burgundy solid, cut four pieces from Template B. Reverse Template B and cut four additional pieces.

3. From the white solid, cut one piece from Template C.

4. From the peach solid, cut four pieces each from Templates D and E.

5. From the gold solid, cut one piece from Template F. (Note that there is no seam allowance because the square is appliquéd with the raw edge exposed.)

Assemble the Block

1. Sew two B triangles to one A shape. Repeat to make a total of four pieced rectangles. (Figure 1)

2. Sew two pieced rectangles to the C square. (Figure 2)

3. Sew two D triangles to one pieced rectangle. Repeat to make a second pieced shape. (Figure 3)

4. Sew the pieced shapes to the center strip. (Figure 4)

5. Sew the E triangles to the square center to complete the block. (Figure 5)

6. Refer to the General Instructions for Embroidery (page 8) and use a back stitch to appliqué the F square to the center of the flower. (Figure 6)

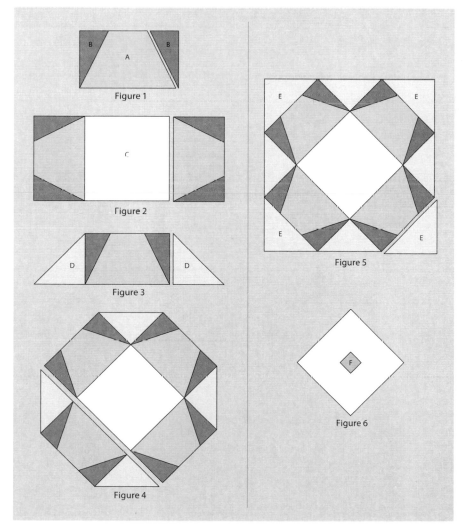

Figure 1

Figure 2

Figure 3

Figure 4

Figure 5

Figure 6

DAFFODIL

Block sizes

6½" square or 8" square

Templates on page 75; enlarge 200%

Fabrics and Materials

Cream solid, yellow pin dot, green solid, purple print, and gold solid

Coordinating thread

Orange embroidery floss

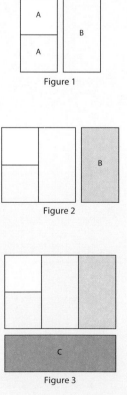

Figure 1

Figure 2

Figure 3

Cut the Pieces

1. From the cream solid, cut four pieces from Template A.

2. From the yellow pin dot, cut four pieces each from Templates A, B, E, and F.

3. From the green solid, cut four pieces from Template B.

4. From the purple print, cut four pieces each from Templates C and D.

5. From the gold solid, cut one piece from Template G.

Assemble the Block

1. Sew one cream A square to one yellow A square; sew this pieced rectangle to one yellow B rectangle to make a square. (Figure 1)

2. Sew one green B rectangle to the pieced square. (Figure 2)

3. Sew one C rectangle to the pieced rectangle. (Figure 3)

4. Repeat steps 1 through 3 to make a total of four pieced squares.

5. Sew one E triangle to one D shape. (Figure 4)

6. Sew one F triangle to the pieced shape you made in step 5. (Figure 5)

7. Repeat steps 5 and 6 to make a total of four pieced rectangles.

8. Sew two pieced rectangles to the G square. (Figure 6)

9. Sew two pieced squares from step 4 to one pieced rectangle from step 6. Repeat to make a second strip. (Figure 7)

10. Sew the strips to the central rectangle created in step 8 to complete the block. (Figure 8)

11. Refer to the General Instructions for Embroidery (page 8) and use a long stitch to make the X marks in the center of the block. (Figure 9)

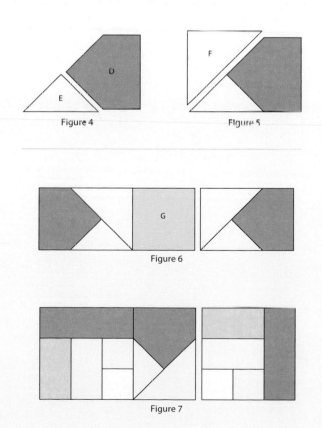

Figure 4

Figure 5

Figure 6

Figure 7

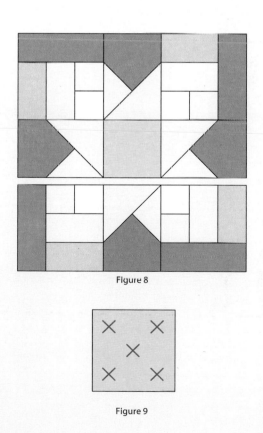

Figure 8

Figure 9

ROSE CORSAGE

Block sizes

7" square or 8½" square

Templates on page 76; enlarge 200%

Fabrics and Materials

Magenta solid, light blue solid, melon solid, pink polka dot, green print, blue polka dot, and purple solid

Coordinating thread

Cut the Pieces

1. From the magenta solid, cut one piece from Template A.

2. From the light blue solid, cut one piece each from Templates A, E, and B. Reverse Template B and cut one additional piece.

3. From the melon solid, cut one piece from Template B. Reverse Template B and cut one additional shape.

4. From the pink polka dot, cut one piece from Template C.

5. From the green print, cut two pieces from Template D.

6. From the blue polka dot, cut four pieces from Template F.

7. From the purple solid, cut four pieces from Template G.

Assemble the Block

1. Sew two A triangles together. (Figure 1)

2. Sew one melon B shape to one light blue B shape. Make a second pieced strip using the pieces cut when you reversed the templates. (Figure 2)

3. Sew the C square, the D rectangles, and the E square together to make a square. (Figure 3)

4. Sew one pieced strip from step 2 to the pieced square. (Figure 4)

5. Sew the pieced square from step 1 to the other pieced strip from step 2. (Figure 5)

6. Sew the new pieced strip to the piece created in step 4 to complete the central square. (Figure 6)

7. Sew one F triangle to one G shape. Repeat to make a total of four pieced triangles. (Figure 7)

8. Sew the pieced triangles to the square center to complete the block. (Figure 8)

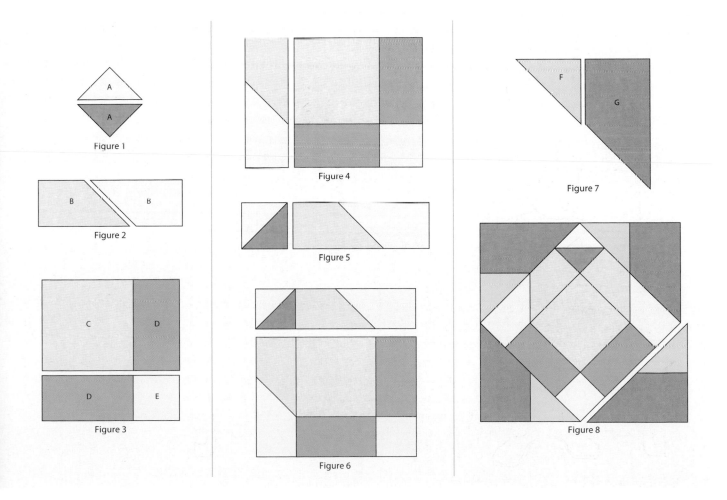

Figure 1

Figure 2

Figure 3

Figure 4

Figure 5

Figure 6

Figure 7

Figure 8

9 FLAME AZALEA

Block sizes

7½" square or 8¾" square

Templates on page 76; enlarge 200%

Fabrics and Materials

Magenta print, yellow print, white solid, and green print

Coordinating thread

4 buttons, ³⁄₈" in diameter

Cut the Pieces

1. From the magenta print, cut one piece from Template A and eight pieces from Template C.

2. From the yellow print, cut four pieces from Template B.

3. From the white solid, cut four pieces each from Templates C and D. Reverse Template D and cut four additional pieces.

4. From the green print, cut one piece from Template E. (Note that the seam allowance is narrow. Because the shape is appliquéd, the edge is turned under at the broken line.)

Assemble the Block

1. Refer to the General Instructions for Curve Patch Piecing (page 8) and sew the B shapes to the A shape to create the central square. (Figure 1)

2. Sew one magenta C shape to one white C shape. Sew one magenta C shape to the other side of the white C shape. (Figure 2)

3. Sew two D shapes to the ends of one pieced strip. Repeat to make a total of four pieced strips. (Figure 3)

4. Refer to the General Instructions for Mitered Corners (page 7), and center a pieced strip on the square center. Starting and stopping ¼" from the fabric edges, sew the strip to the square. (Figure 4)

5. Repeat step 4 with an adjoining side. (Figure 5)

6. Matching the opposite corners, make a diagonal fold and sew the strip ends together. (Figure 6)

7. Trim the seam allowance to ¼". (Figure 7)

8. Repeat steps 5 through 7 to add the remaining strips and complete the block. (Figure 8)

9. Refer to the General Instructions for Hand Appliqué (page 7) and sew the E square to the center of the block. Sew the buttons in place at each corner of the E square. (Figure 9)

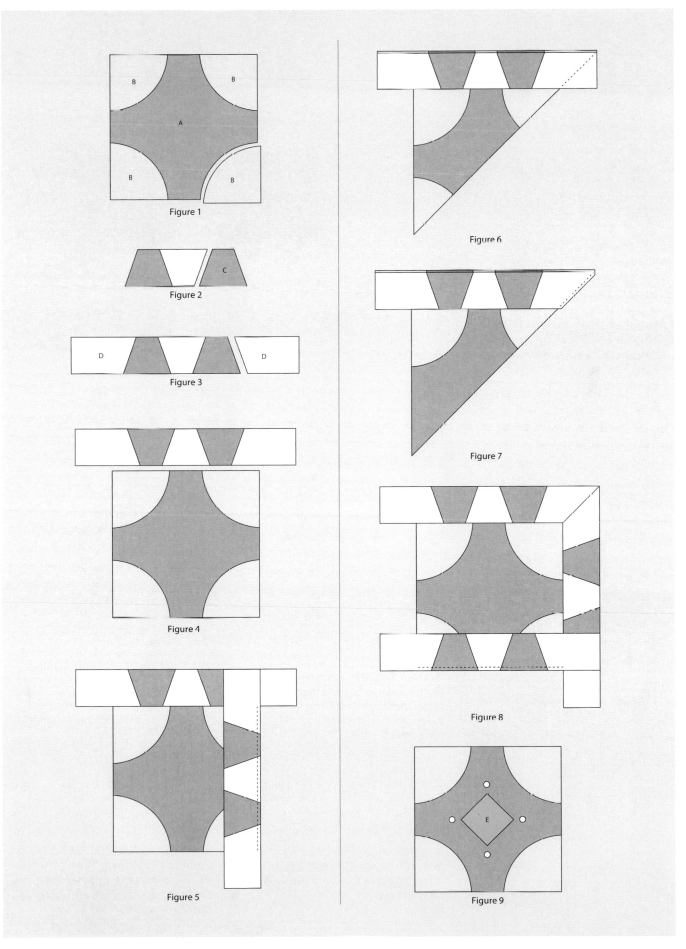

Figure 1

Figure 2

Figure 3

Figure 4

Figure 5

Figure 6

Figure 7

Figure 8

Figure 9

SWEET CAMELLIA

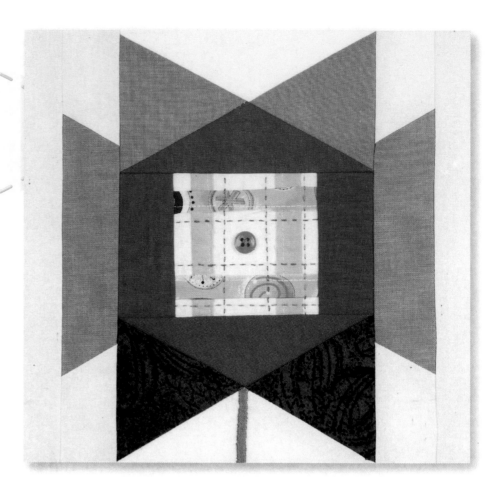

Block sizes

7½" square or 9" square

Templates on page 77; enlarge 200%

Fabrics and Materials

White solid, magenta solid, melon solid, cream solid, and dark green print

Coordinating thread

Blue and lime bias trim

Pink and green embroidery floss

1 button, ⅜" in diameter

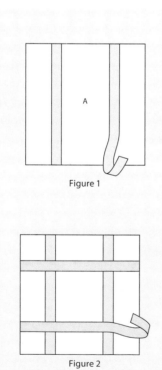

Figure 1

Figure 2

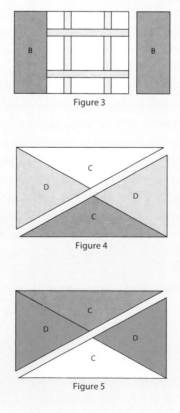

Figure 3

Figure 4

Figure 5

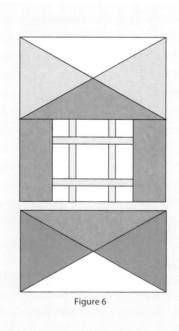

Figure 6

Figure 7

Cut the Pieces

1. From the white solid, cut one piece from Template A and two pieces from Template C.

2. From the magenta solid, cut two pieces each from Templates B and C.

3. From the melon solid, cut two pieces each from Templates D and F.

4. From the cream solid, cut two pieces from Template E. Reverse Template E and cut two additional pieces. For a 7½" block, cut two 1½" x 8" strips. For a 9" block, cut two 1⅜" x 9½" strips.

5. From the dark green print, cut two pieces from Template D.

Assemble the Block

1. Center and sew two pieces of blue trim to the A square. (Figure 1)

2. Center and sew two pieces of lime trim to the A square. (Figure 2)

3. Sew the B rectangles to two sides of the A square. (Figure 3)

4. Sew one white C triangle to one white D triangle. Sew one magenta C triangle to one white D triangle. (Figure 4)

5. Sew one magenta C triangle to one green D triangle. Sew one white C triangle to one green D triangle. (Figure 5)

6. Sew the pieced rectangles to the square center. (Figure 6)

7. Sew two E shapes to the ends of one F shape. Repeat to make a second pieced strip. (Figure 7)

8. Sew the pieced strips to the center rectangle. (Figure 8)

9. Sew the cream strips to the square center to complete the block. (Figure 9)

10. Refer to the General Instructions for Embroidery (page 8) and use a satin stitch to make the stem. (Figure 10)

11. Use a running stitch to make the vertical and horizontal lines. Then sew the button in the center of the block. (Figure 11)

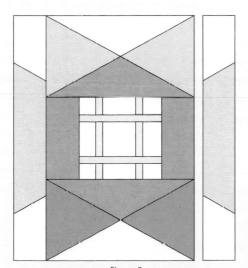

Figure 8

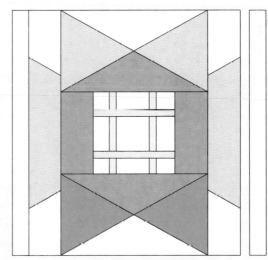

Figure 9

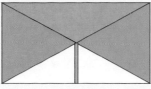

Figure 10

Figure 11

11 DOGWOOD

Block sizes

7½" square or 9" square

Templates on page 77; enlarge 200%

Fabrics and Materials

Gold print, white solid, green print, and blue solid

Coordinating thread

Cut the Pieces

1. From the gold print, cut four pieces from Template A.

2. From the white solid, cut four pieces from Template B.

3. From the green print, cut eight pieces from Template A and four pieces from Template C.

4. From the blue solid, cut four pieces each from Templates D and E.

Assemble the Block

1. Sew one gold A triangle to one B shape. Repeat to make a total of four pieced shapes. (Figure 1)

2. Sew the pieced shapes together. (Figure 2)

3. Sew the C triangles to the corners of the pieced shape. (Figure 3)

4. Sew one green A triangle to one D shape. (Figure 4)

5. Sew one green A triangle to one E shape. (Figure 5)

6. Sew the pieced shapes from steps 4 and 5 together. Repeat to make a total of four pieced strips. (Figure 6)

7. Refer to the General Instructions for the Log Cabin Border (page 7), and sew the pieced strips to the central square to complete the block. (Figure 7)

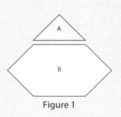

Figure 1

Figure 2

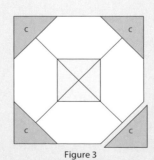

Figure 3

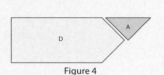

Figure 4

Figure 5

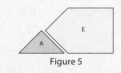

Figure 6

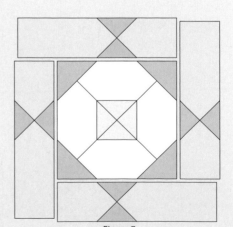

Figure 7

12 BLUE ASTER

Block sizes
7½" square or 9" square

Templates on page 78; enlarge 200%

Fabrics and Materials
Yellow print, turquoise print, turquoise solid, and white solid

Coordinating thread

Cut the Pieces

1. From the yellow print, cut one piece from Template A.

2. From the turquoise print, cut four pieces from Template B.

3. From the turquoise solid, cut four pieces from Template C and eight pieces from Template E.

4. From the white solid, cut four pieces each from Templates D and E. Reverse Template D and cut four additional pieces.

Assemble the Block

1. Sew the B triangles to the A square. (Figure 1)

2. Sew one D shape to one C triangle. Trim the overlapping corner. (Figure 2 & Figure 3)

3. Sew a reverse D shape to the pieced shape. (Figure 4)

4. Sew two turquoise E triangles to the pieced shape. (Figure 5)

5. Repeat steps 2 through 4 to make a total of four pieced shapes.

6. Sew two pieced shapes to the square center. (Figure 6)

7. Sew two white E triangles to one remaining pieced shape. Repeat with the remaining pieced shape. (Figure 7)

8. Sew the pieced triangles to the square center to complete the block. (Figure 8)

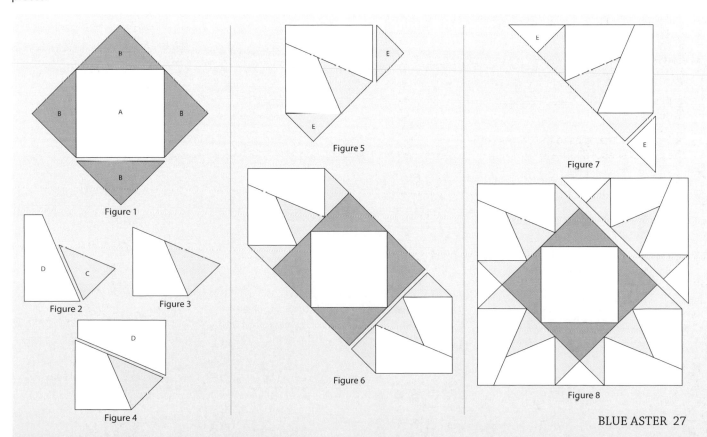

Figure 1

Figure 2

Figure 3

Figure 4

Figure 5

Figure 6

Figure 7

Figure 8

BLUE ASTER 27

HIBISCUS

13

Block sizes

7½" square or 9" square

Templates on page 78; enlarge 200%

Fabrics and Materials

Cream solid, orange print, red print, blue solid, mint solid, lime print

Coordinating thread

Lime green, and orange embroidery floss

Cut the Pieces

1. From the cream solid, cut one piece from Template A.

2. From the orange print, cut two pieces from Template B and four pieces from Template E.

3. From the red print, cut one piece from Template A.

4. From the blue solid, cut two pieces from Template D, four pieces from Template F, and one piece each from Templates G and C. Reverse Template C and cut an additional piece.

5. From the mint solid, cut two pieces from Template F and one piece from Template C. Reverse Template C and cut an additional piece.

6. From the lime print, cut one piece from Template H. (Note that the seam allowance is narrow. Because the shape is appliquéd, the edge is turned under at the broken line.)

Assemble the Block

1. Sew the cream A diamond to one B triangle. (Figure 1)

2. Sew the blue C triangles to the pieced shape. (Figure 2)

3. Sew the red A diamond to one B triangle. (Figure 3)

4. Sew the mint C triangles to the pieced shape. (Figure 4)

5. Sew the pieced shapes together to create a rectangle. (Figure 5)

6. Sew one D triangle to two E triangles. (Figure 6)

7. Sew two blue F squares to the ends of the pieced rectangle. (Figure 7)

8. Repeat steps 6 and 7 to make a second pieced strip.

9. Sew the strips to the sides of the rectangular center. (Figure 8)

10. Sew the mint F squares to the outsides of the G rectangle. (Figure 9)

11. Sew the pieced strip to the bottom of the square created in step 9. (Figure 10)

12. Refer to the General Instructions for Hand Appliqué (page 7) and sew the H shape in place. Refer to the General Instructions for Embroidery (page 8) and use a wrapped back stitch to make the arc. Use a running stitch to make the rays, and use a blanket stitch to outline the edge. (Figure 11)

13. Use a satin stitch to make the stem. (Figure 12)

Figure 1

Figure 2

Figure 3

Figure 4

Figure 5

Figure 6

Figure 7

Figure 8

Figure 9

Figure 10

Figure 11

Figure 12

14 POINSETTIA

Block sizes

7½" square or 8¾" square

Templates on page 79; enlarge 200%

Fabrics and Materials

Red print, yellow solid, white solid, and green solid

Coordinating thread

Green embroidery floss

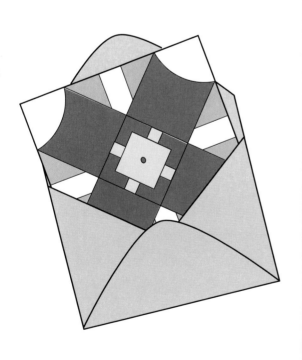

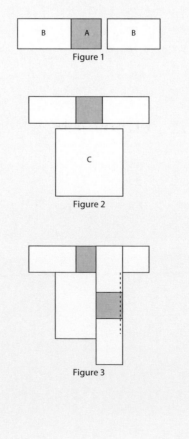

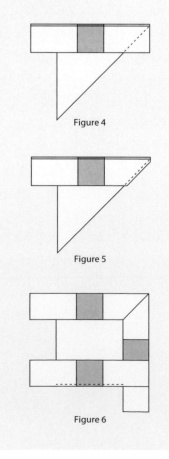

Cut the Pieces

1. From the red print, cut four pieces each from Templates A and D.

2. From the yellow solid, cut eight pieces from Template B and one piece from Template C.

3. From the white solid, cut four pieces each from Templates E and F.

4. From the green solid, cut eight pieces from Template G.

Assemble the Block

1. Sew two B rectangles to the ends of one A square. Repeat to make a total of four pieced strips. (Figure 1)

2. Refer to the General Instructions for Mitered Corners (page 7), and center one pieced strip on the C square. Starting and stopping ¼" from the fabric edges, sew the strip to the square. (Figure 2)

3. Repeat step 2 with the adjoining side. (Figure 3)

4. Matching opposite corners, make a diagonal fold and sew the strip ends together. (Figure 4)

5. Trim the seam allowance to ¼". (Figure 5)

6. Repeat steps 2 through 5 to complete the square center. (Figure 6)

7. Refer to the General Instructions for Curve Patch Piecing (page 8) and sew one E shape to one D shape. Repeat to make a total of four pieced shapes. (Figure 7)

8. Sew two pieced shapes to the square center. (Figure 8). Sew two G triangles to one F shape. Repeat to make a total of four pieced triangles. (Figure 9)

9. Sew two pieced triangles to one pieced shape from step 7. Repeat with the remaining triangles and shape. (Figure 10)

10. Sew the pieced triangles to the square center to complete the block. (Figure 11)

11. Refer to the General Instructions for Embroidery (page 8) and use the spider web rose stitch to make the center flower. Use the long stitch to make the leaves. (Figure 12)

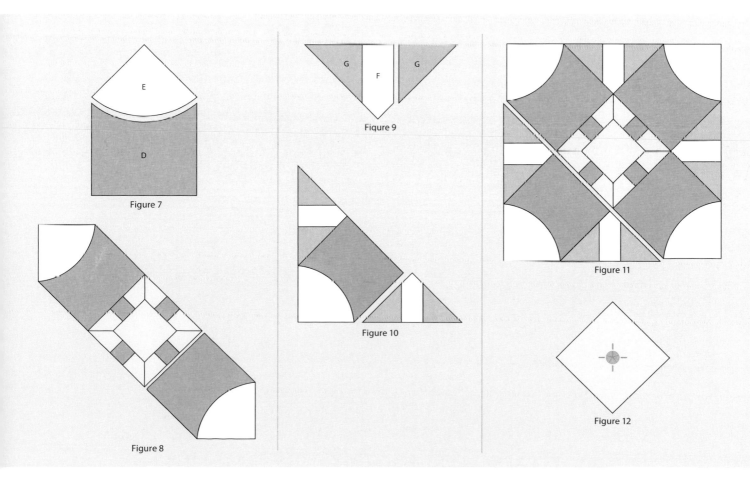

Figure 7

Figure 8

Figure 9

Figure 10

Figure 11

Figure 12

15
HONEYSUCKLE

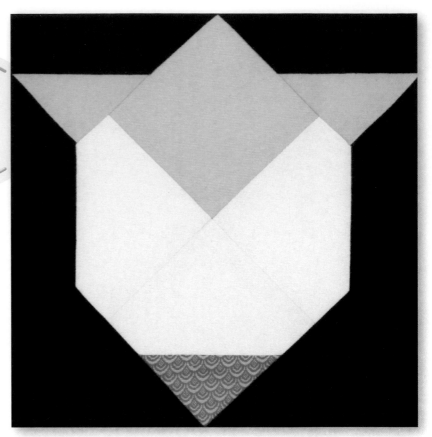

Block sizes
6" square or 7¹/₂" square

Templates on page 79; enlarge 200%

Fabrics and Materials
Gold solid, cream solid, burgundy solid, and green print

Coordinating thread

Cut the Pieces
1. From the gold solid, cut one piece from Template A and two pieces from Template C.

2. From the cream solid, cut three pieces from Template B.

3. From the burgundy solid, cut four pieces from Template C, two pieces from Template D, and two pieces from Template E.

4. From the green print, cut one piece from Template C.

Assemble the Block
1. Sew the green C triangle to one B shape. Sew the burgundy C triangles to the remaining B shapes. (Figure 1)

2. Sew the pieced squares to the A square. (Figure 2)

3. Sew one burgundy C triangle to one gold C triangle. Sew the pieced triangle to one D shape to form a larger triangle. Make a second pieced triangle that is the reverse. (Figure 3)

4. Sew the pieced triangles and the E triangles to the square center to complete the block. (Figure 4)

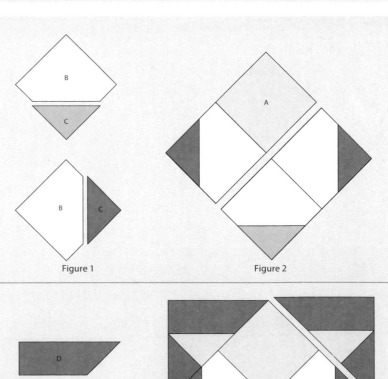

Figure 1

Figure 2

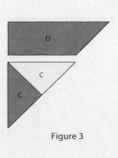

Figure 3

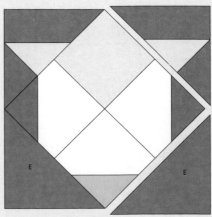

Figure 4

Block sizes

7¹/₂" square or 9" square

Templates on page 80; enlarge 200%

Fabrics and Materials

Yellow solid, lavender solid, purple mottle, olive print, and orange polka dot

Coordinating thread

Cut the Pieces

1. From the yellow solid, cut one piece from Template A.

2. From the lavender solid, cut four pieces from Template B.

3. From the purple mottle, cut four pieces each from Templates C and E.

4. From the olive print, cut four pieces each from Templates D and F.

5. From the orange polka dot: for a 7¹/₂" block, cut four strips, each ³/₈" x 7¹/₄"; for a 9" block, cut four strips, each 1¹/₂" x 8¹/₂".

Assemble the Block

1. Sew the B triangles to the A square. (Figure 1)

2. Sew one C triangle to one D triangle. (Figure 2)

3. Sew one E triangle to the pieced shape. Repeat to make a total of four pieced strips. (Figure 3)

4. Sew two pieced strips to the sides of the square center. (Figure 4)

5. Sew the F squares to the ends of the remaining strips. (Figure 5)

6. Sew the remaining strips to the square center to complete the block. (Figure 6)

7. Refer to the General Instructions for the Log Cabin Border (page 7), and sew the orange print strips to the outside of the square to complete the block. (Figure 7)

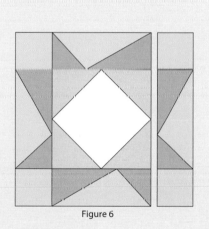

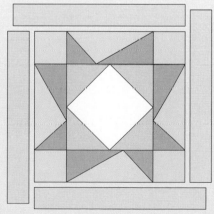

Figure 1

Figure 2

Figure 3

Figure 4

Figure 5

Figure 6

Figure 7

17 BLUE BONNET

Block sizes
7" square or 8½" square

Templates on page 80; enlarge 200%

Fabrics and Materials
Teal solid, purple solid, ivory mottle, and yellow print

Coordinating thread

Cut the Pieces
1. From the teal solid, cut two pieces from Template A. Reverse Template A and cut two additional pieces.

2. From the purple solid, cut two pieces from Template A. Reverse Template A and cut two additional pieces.

3. From the ivory mottle, cut four pieces from Template B. Reverse Template B and cut four additional pieces. Cut eight pieces from Template C.

4. From the yellow print, cut four pieces from Template C.

Assemble the Block
1. Sew one B triangle to one A shape. (Figure 1)

2. Sew one ivory C triangle to the pieced shape. Repeat to make a total of four pieced shapes (two teal and two purple). Make four additional pieced shapes using the pieces cut when you reversed the templates. (Figure 2)

3. Sew one pieced teal shape to one reverse-pieced purple shape. Repeat to make a total of four pieced shapes. (Figure 3)

4. Sew one yellow C triangle to one pieced shape. Repeat to make a total of four pieced squares. (Figure 4)

5. Sew the squares together to complete the block. (Figure 5)

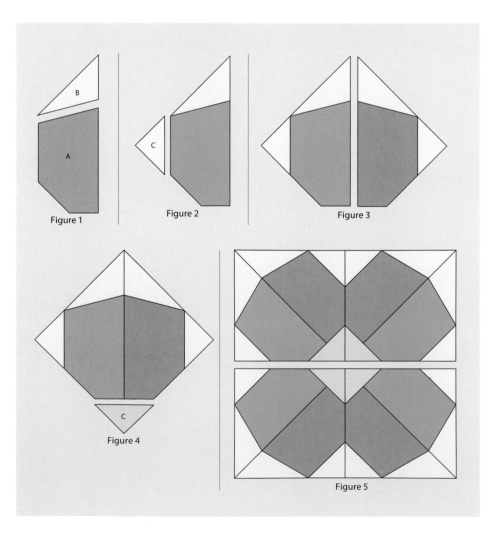

Figure 1

Figure 2

Figure 3

Figure 4

Figure 5

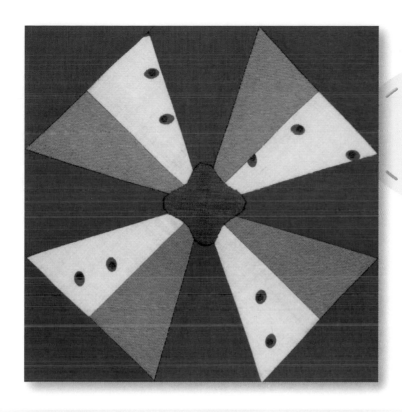

Block sizes

6¾" square or 8" square

Templates on page 81; enlarge 200%

Fabrics and Materials

Teal solid, melon solid, yellow print, and dark pink solid

Coordinating thread

Cut the Pieces

1. From the teal solid, cut four pieces each from Templates A and C.

2. From the melon solid, cut four pieces from Template B.

3. From the yellow print, reverse Template B and cut four additional pieces.

4. From the dark pink solid, cut one piece from Template D. (Note that the seam allowance is narrow. Because the shape is appliquéd, the edge is turned under at the broken line.)

Assemble the Block

1. Sew one melon B triangle to one yellow print B triangle. Sew one A triangle to the pieced triangle to create a kite shape. Repeat to make a total of four pieced kite shapes. (Figure 1)

2. Sew one C triangle to one pieced kite shape. Repeat to make a total of four pieced shapes. (Figure 2)

3. Sew the pieced shapes together to complete the block. (Figure 3 & Figure 4)

4. Refer to the General Instructions for Hand Appliqué (page 7) and sew the D shape to the square center. (Figure 5)

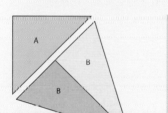

Figure 1

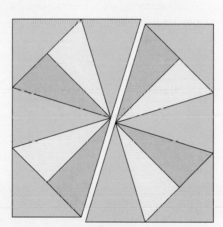

Figure 4

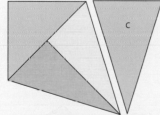

Figure 2

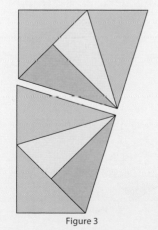

Figure 3

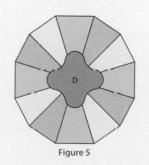

Figure 5

SWEET PEA

Block sizes
7" square or 8½" square

Templates on page 81;
enlarge 200%

Fabrics and Materials
Orange print, navy print, tan print, green print, lime solid, and yellow solid

Coordinating thread

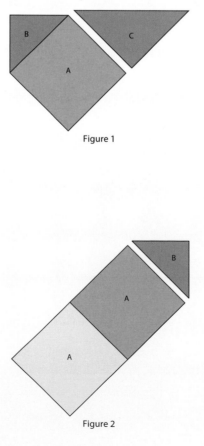

Figure 1

Figure 2

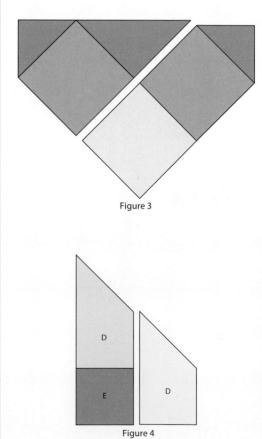

Figure 3

Figure 4

Cut the Pieces

1. From the orange print, cut two pieces from Template A.

2. From the navy print, cut two pieces each from Templates B and E, and one piece from Template C.

3. From the tan print, cut one piece from Template A.

4. From the green print, cut one piece from Template D. Reverse Template D and cut an additional piece.

5. From the lime solid, cut one piece from Template D. Reverse Template D and cut an additional piece.

6. From the yellow solid: for a 7" block, cut four strips, each 1¾" x 6½"; for an 8½" block, cut four strips, each 2" x 8¼".

Assemble the Block

1. Sew one B triangle and one C triangle to one orange print A square. (Figure 1)

2. Sew one tan print A square to one orange print A square. Sew a B triangle to the pieced rectangle. (Figure 2)

3. Sew the pieced shapes together to form a triangular shape. (Figure 3)

4. Sew one E square to one green print D shape. Sew the pieced shape to one lime solid D shape. Make a second pieced shape using the pieces cut when you reversed the templates. (Figure 4)

5. Starting and stopping ¼" from the fabric edges, sew one pieced shape to the flower top. (Figure 5)

6. Starting and stopping ¼" from the fabric edges, sew the other pieced shape created in step 4 to the flower top. (Figure 6)

7. Align the lime solid D shapes, and starting and stopping ¼" from the fabric edges, sew the D shapes together. (Figure 7)

8. Refer to the General Instructions for the Log Cabin Border (page 7), and sew the yellow solid strips to the outside of the square to complete the block. (Figure 8)

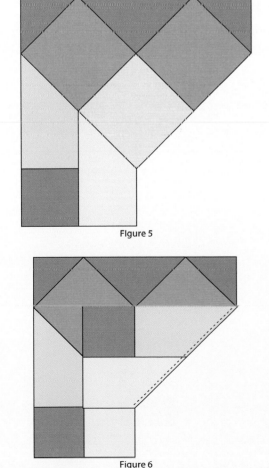

Figure 5

Figure 6

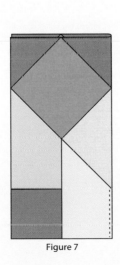

Figure 7

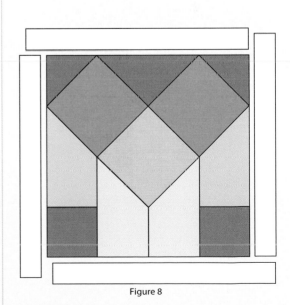

Figure 8

ROSE OF SHARON

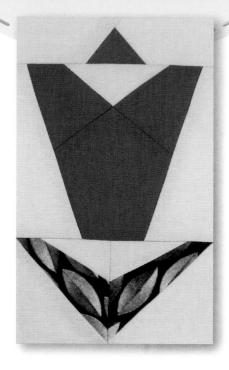

Block sizes

5" x 8" rectangle or
6¼" x 10" rectangle

Templates on page 82; enlarge 200%

Fabrics and Materials

Rose solid, peach solid, and green print

Coordinating thread

Cut the Pieces

1. From the rose solid, cut one piece each from Templates A, D, and E. Reverse the D template and cut a second piece.

2. From the peach solid, cut one piece each from Templates C, B, F, G, and I. Reverse Templates B, F, G, and I and cut a second piece from each.

3. From the green print, cut one piece from Template H. Reverse Template H and cut a second piece.

Assemble the Block

1. Sew the A triangle to the B shape. Trim the overlapping corner. (Figure 1 & Figure 2)

2. Sew the remaining B shape to the pieced shape. (Figure 3)

3. Sew one D shape to the C triangle. Sew the E shape to the remaining D shape. Sew the pieced shapes together. (Figure 4)

4. Sew the F shapes to the piece created in step 3 to make a square center. (Figure 5)

5. Sew one G triangle to one H shape. Sew one I shape to the pieced shape. Make a second pieced square that is the reverse. (Figure 6)

6. Sew the pieced squares together. (Figure 7)

7. Sew the pieced rectangles to the square center to complete the block. (Figure 8)

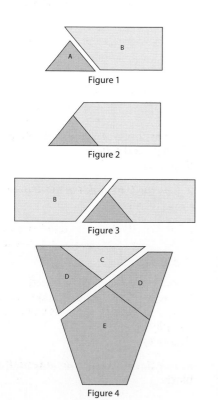

Figure 1

Figure 2

Figure 3

Figure 4

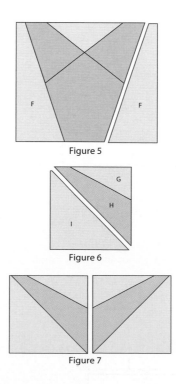

Figure 5

Figure 6

Figure 7

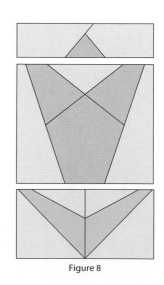

Figure 8

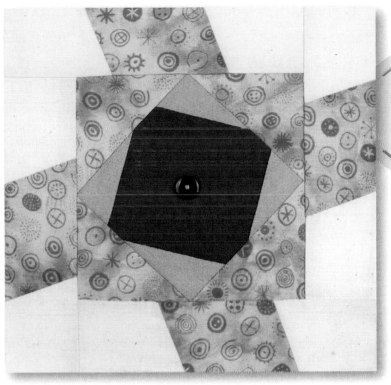

Block sizes

7" square or 9" square

Templates on page 83;
enlarge 200%

Fabrics and Materials

Purple solid, pink solid, blue print, and cream solid

Coordinating thread

1 coordinating button, ½" in diameter

Cut the Pieces

1. From the purple solid, cut one piece from Template A.

2. From the pink solid, cut four pieces from Template B.

3. From the blue print, cut four pieces from Template C and four pieces from Template E.

4. From the cream solid, cut eight pieces from Template D.

Assemble the Block

1. Matching the corners to the Xs, sew the B triangles to the A square. Trim the corners flush with the edges of the pieced square.
(Figure 1)

2. Sew the C triangles to the square center. (Figure 2)

3. Sew two D shapes to one E shape. Repeat to make a total of four pieced strips. (Figure 3)

4. Refer to the General Instructions for the Log Cabin Border (page 7), and sew the pieced strips to the square to complete the block.
(Figure 4)

5. Sew the button to the center of the block.

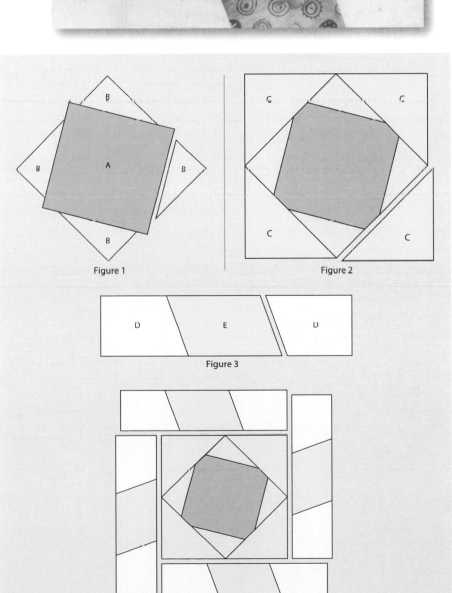

Figure 1

Figure 2

Figure 3

Figure 4

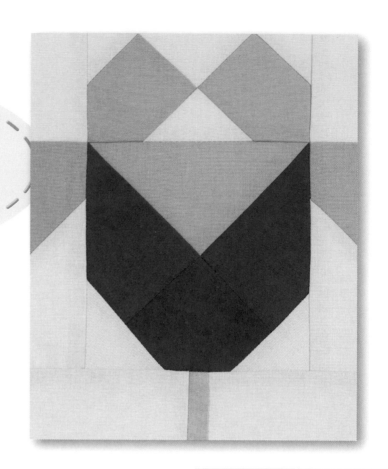

22 DUTCH IRIS

Block sizes

7" x 8" rectangle or 8¼" x 9⅜" rectangle

Templates on page 84; enlarge 200%

Fabrics and Materials

Periwinkle solid, peach solid, dark blue solid, and green solid

Coordinating thread

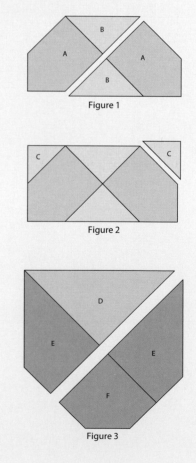

Figure 1

Figure 2

Figure 3

Cut the Pieces

1. From the periwinkle solid, cut two pieces from Template A, and one piece each from Templates D and H. Reverse Template H and cut an additional piece.

2. From the peach solid, cut four pieces from Template B, two pieces each from Templates C, G, and J, and one piece from Template I. Reverse Template I and cut an additional piece.

3. From the dark blue solid, cut two pieces from Template E and one piece from Template F.

4. From the green solid, cut one piece from Template K.

Assemble the Block

1. Sew the one A shape to one B triangle. Sew the remaining A shape to the remaining B triangle. Sew the pieced shapes together. (Figure 1)

2. Sew the C triangles to the pieced shape to create a rectangle. (Figure 2)

3. Sew one E shape to the D triangle. Sew the remaining E shape to the F shape. Sew the pieced shapes together. (Figure 3)

4. Sew the remaining B triangles to the pieced shape to create a square. (Figure 4)

5. Sew the pieced rectangle to the pieced square. (Figure 5)

6. Sew one H shape to one I shape. Sew one G rectangle to the top of the pieced strip. Using the pieces cut when you reversed the templates, make another pieced strip. (Figure 6)

7. Sew the pieced strips to the flower center. (Figure 7)

8. Sew the J rectangles to the sides of the K rectangle. (Figure 8)

9. Sew the pieced strip to the square center to complete the block. (Figure 9)

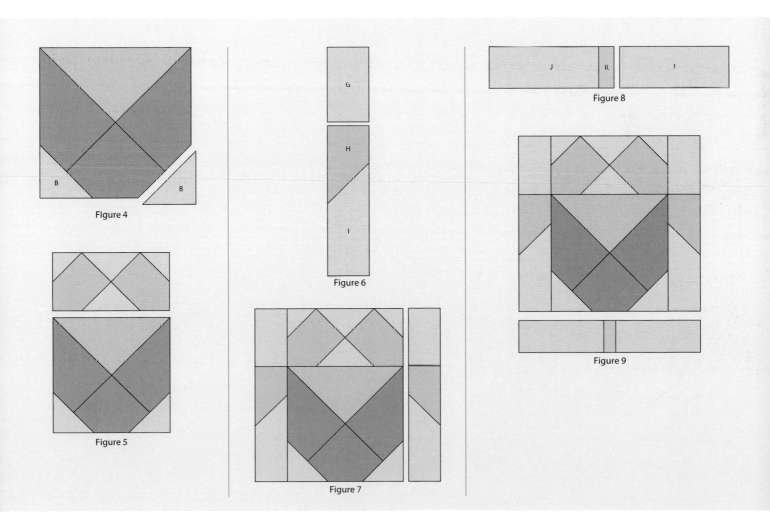

Figure 4

Figure 5

Figure 6

Figure 7

Figure 8

Figure 9

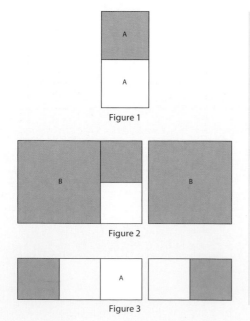

ANEMONE

Block sizes

6¼" square or 7¾" square

Templates on page 85; enlarge 200%

Fabrics and Materials

Navy print, yellow print, white solid, and purple print

Coordinating thread

4 buttons, each ¼" in diameter

Cut the Pieces

1. From the navy print, cut four pieces each from Templates A and B.

2. From the yellow print, cut four pieces from Template A.

3. From the white solid, cut one piece from Template A.

4. From the purple print, cut four pieces from Template C. (Note that the seam allowance is narrow. Because the shapes are appliquéd, the edges are turned under at the broken line.)

Assemble the Block

1. Sew one navy A square to one yellow A square. Repeat to make a total of four pieced rectangles. (Figure 1)

2. Sew two B squares to one pieced rectangle. Repeat to make a second pieced rectangle. (Figure 2)

3. Sew the remaining pieced rectangles to two sides of the white A square. (Figure 3)

4. Sew the pieced strips together to complete the block. (Figure 4)

5. Refer to the General Instructions for Hand Appliqué (page 7) and sew the C shapes to the corner squares. Sew the buttons in place at the corners of the flower center. (Figure 5)

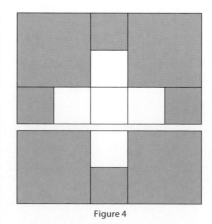

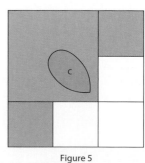

Figure 1

Figure 2

Figure 3

Figure 4

Figure 5

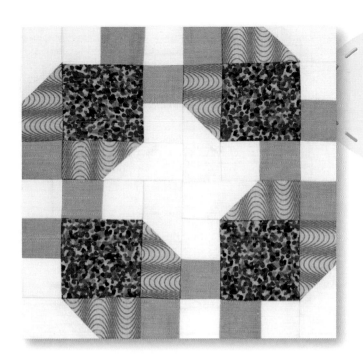

GARDEN TRELLIS

Block sizes

8" square or 9½" square

Templates on page 85;
enlarge 200%

Fabrics and Materials

Dark pink print, cream solid,
green solid, and light pink print

Coordinating thread

Cut the Pieces

1. From the dark pink print, cut four pieces from Template A.

2. From the cream solid, cut twelve pieces from Template B and four pieces from Template C. Reverse Template C and cut four additional pieces.

3. From the green solid, cut twelve pieces from Template B.

4. From the light pink print, cut four pieces from Template C. Reverse Template C and cut four additional pieces.

Assemble the Block

1. Sew one cream B square to one green B square. Sew the pieced rectangle to one A square. (Figure 1)

2. Sew two cream B squares to the sides of one green B square. (Figure 2)

3. Sew the pieced strip to the pieced rectangle created in step 1. (Figure 3)

4. Sew one pink C shape to one cream C shape. Make a second pieced strip using the pieces cut when you reversed the templates. (Figure 4)

5. Sew one pieced strip to the pieced square. (Figure 5)

6. Sew one green B square to the top of the remaining pieced strip. (Figure 6)

7. Sew the pieced strip to the pieced shape to create a square. (Figure 7)

8. Repeat steps 1 through 7 to make a total of four squares.

9. Sew the pieced squares together to complete the block. (Figure 8)

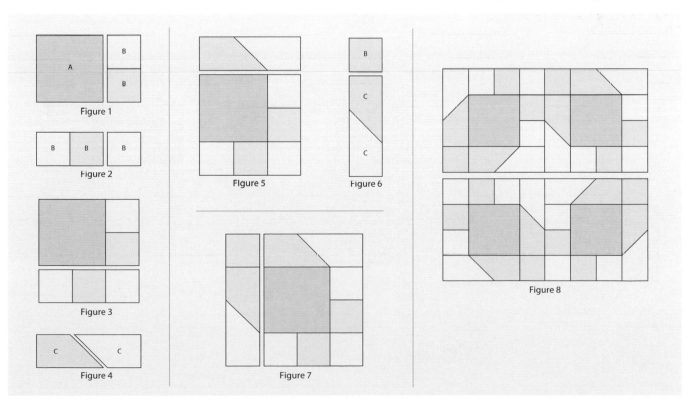

Figure 1

Figure 2

Figure 3

Figure 4

Figure 5

Figure 6

Figure 7

Figure 8

25

PASSION FLOWER

Block sizes

7½" square or 9" square

Templates on page 86; enlarge 200%

Fabrics and Materials

White solid, periwinkle solid, purple solid, violet print, dark blue print, yellow pin dot, and light blue solid

Coordinating thread

4 contrasting buttons, ¼" in diameter

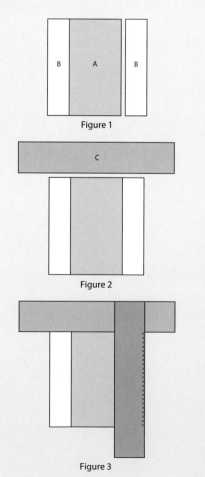

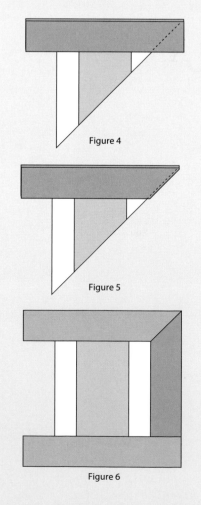

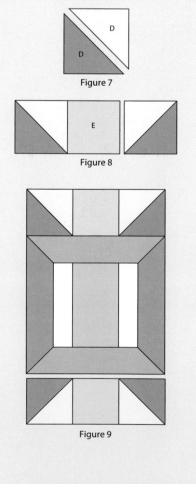

Cut the Pieces

1. From the periwinkle solid, cut one piece from Template A.

2. From the white solid, cut two pieces from Template B.

3. From the purple solid, cut two pieces from Template C.

4. From the violet print, cut two pieces from Template C.

5. From the dark blue print, cut four pieces from Template D and two pieces from Template F. Reverse Template F and cut two additional pieces.

6. From the yellow pin dot, cut four pieces from Template D, two pieces from Template G, and four pieces from Template E.

7. From the light blue solid, cut two pieces from Template E.

Assemble the Block

1. Sew the A rectangle to the B rectangles to make a square. (Figure 1)

2. Refer to the General Instructions for Mitered Corners (page 7), and center a purple C strip on the square center. Starting and stopping ¼" from the fabric edges, sew the strip to the square. (Figure 2)

3. Repeat step 2, using a violet C strip on the adjoining side of the square. (Figure 3)

4. Matching opposite corners, make a diagonal fold and sew the strip ends together. Trim the seam allowance to ¼". (Figure 4 & Figure 5)

5. Repeat steps 2 through 4 to add the remaining sides and complete the central block. (Figure 6)

6. Sew one blue D triangle to one yellow D triangle. Repeat to make a total of four pieced squares. (Figure 7)

7. Sew two pieced squares to one blue E square. Repeat to make a second pieced strip. (Figure 8)

8. Sew the pieced strips to the center block. (Figure 9)

9. Sew two F shapes to one G triangle. Repeat to make a second pieced strip. (Figure 10)

10. Sew two yellow E squares to the ends of one of the pieced strips created in step 10. Repeat with the second strip. (Figure 11)

11. Sew the pieced strips to the square center to complete the block. (Figure 12)

12. Sew the buttons to the flower center.

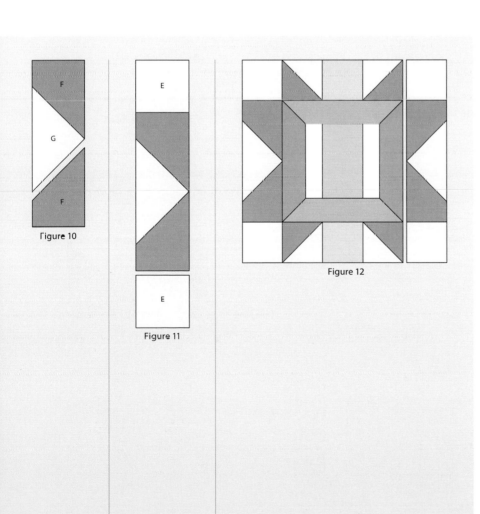

Figure 10

Figure 11

Figure 12

SNAPDRAGON

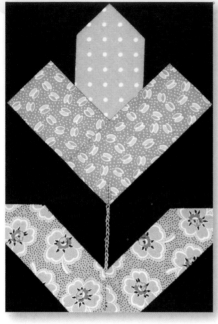

Block sizes

5½" x 8" rectangle or
6¾" x 10¼" rectangle

Templates on page 86;
enlarge 200%

Fabrics and Materials

Pink polka dot, brown solid,
orange print, and green print

Coordinating thread

Green embroidery thread

Cut the Pieces

1. From the pink polka dot, cut one piece from Template A.

2. From the brown solid, cut two pieces from Template B, and four pieces each from Templates E and G.

3. From the orange print, cut one piece each from Templates C and D.

4. From the green print, cut two pieces from Template F.

Assemble the Block

1. Sew the B triangles to the A shape. (Figure 1)

2. Sew the C rectangle to the pieced square. Sew the D rectangle to the pieced square. (Figure 2)

3. Sew the E triangles to the pieced square. (Figure 3)

4. Sew two G triangles to one F shape. Repeat to make a second pieced square. (Figure 4)

5. Sew the pieced squares together. (Figure 5)

6. Sew the pieced rectangle created in step 5 to the square center to complete the block. (Figure 6)

7. Refer to the General Instructions for Embroidery (page 8) and use a chain stitch to make a stem. (Figure 7)

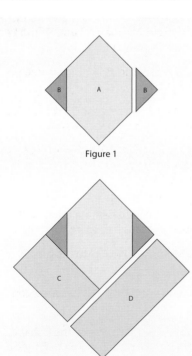

Figure 1

Figure 2

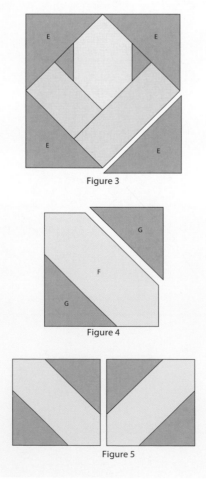

Figure 3

Figure 4

Figure 5

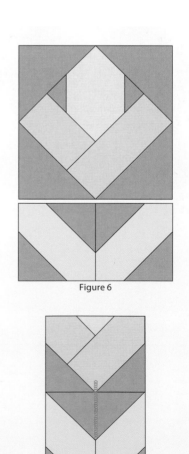

Figure 6

Figure 7

Block sizes

7" square or 9" square

Templates on page 87; enlarge 200%

Fabrics and Materials

Yellow print, cream solid, violet print, green print, and gold print

Coordinating thread

Green embroidery floss

Cut the Pieces

1. From the yellow print, cut one piece from Template A.

2. From the cream solid, cut one piece each from Templates A and D, and two pieces from Template C.

3. From the violet print, cut three pieces from Template B.

4. From the green print, cut one piece each from Templates E and F.

5. From the gold print, cut four pieces from Template G.

Assemble the Block

1. Sew the yellow A triangle to the cream A triangle. (Figure 1)

2. Sew the B squares to the pieced square. (Figure 2)

3. Sew the C triangles to the pieced square. (Figure 3)

4. Sew the D triangle to the E shape. Sew the pieced shape to the F shape. (Figure 4)

5. Sew the two pieced triangles together. (Figure 5)

6. Sew the G triangles to the square center to complete the block. (Figure 6)

7. Refer to the General Instructions for Embroidery (page 8) and use a stem stitch to make the stem. (Figure 7)

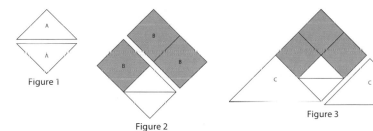

Figure 1

Figure 2

Figure 3

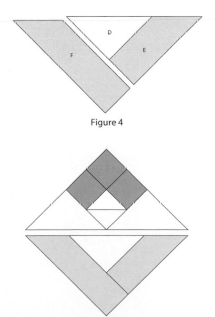

Figure 4

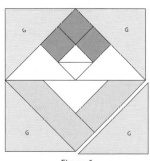

Figure 6

Figure 5

Figure 7

HOLLYHOCK

Block sizes

7" square or 8½" square

Templates on page 87; enlarge 200%

Fabrics and Materials

Red print, turquoise print, green solid, and yellow pin dot

Coordinating thread

Green embroidery floss

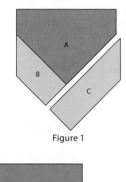

Figure 1

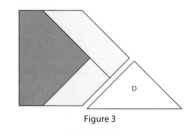

Figure 3

Figure 2

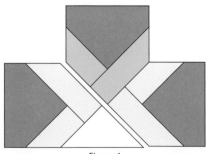

Figure 4

Cut the Pieces

1. From the red print, cut three pieces from Template A.

2. From the turquoise print, cut one piece each from Templates B and C.

3. From the green solid, cut two pieces each from Templates B and C.

4. From the yellow pin dot, cut one piece from Template D and two pieces from Template E. For a 7" block, cut one 2½" x 7½" rectangle. For an 8½" block, cut one 3" x 9" rectangle.

Assemble the Block

1. Sew the turquoise B shape to one A shape. Sew the turquoise C shape to the pieced shape. Repeat with the remaining A, the green B, and the green C shapes to make a total of three pieced shapes. (Figure 1)

2. Starting and stopping ¼" from the fabric edges, sew two pieced shapes together. (Figure 2)

3. Sew the D triangle to one pieced shape. (Figure 3)

4. Starting and stopping ¼" from the fabric edges, sew the pieced shapes together. (Figure 4)

5. Starting and stopping ¼" from the fabric edges, sew one E square to one pieced shape. (Figure 5)

6. Align the adjoining side of the E square with the horizontal pieced shape and, starting and stopping ¼" from the fabric edges, sew the shapes together. (Figure 6 & Figure 7)

7. Repeat steps 5 and 6 with the opposite corner. (Figure 8)

8. Sew the yellow rectangle to the pieced shape to complete the block. (Figure 9)

9. Refer to the General Instructions for Embroidery (page 8) and use a back stitch to make the stems. (Figure 10)

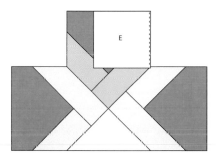

Figure 5

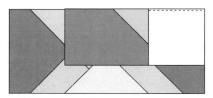

Figure 6

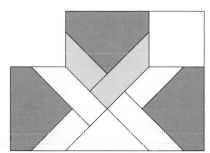

Figure 7

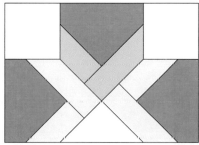

Figure 8

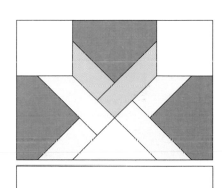

Figure 9

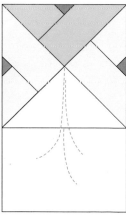

Figure 10

29 CALLA LILIES

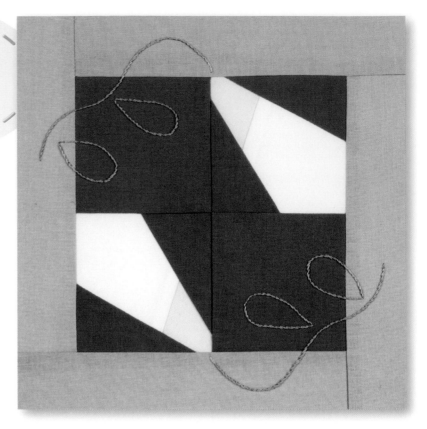

Block sizes

7½" square or 9" square

Templates on page 88; enlarge 200%

Fabrics and Materials

White solid, mint solid, brown solid, and mauve solid

Coordinating thread

Sage embroidery floss

Cut the Pieces

1. From the white solid, cut two pieces from Template A.

2. From the mint solid, cut two pieces from Template B.

3. From the brown solid, cut two pieces each from Templates C and D. Reverse Template C and cut two additional pieces.

4. From the mauve solid: for a 7½" block, cut four strips, each 1¼" x 7¼"; for a 9" block, cut four strips, each 1½" x 8¾".

Assemble the Block

1. Sew one white A shape to one green B shape. (Figure 1)

2. Sew one regular C triangle and one reverse C triangle to the pieced shape to create a square. (Figure 2)

3. Sew one D square to one pieced square. (Figure 3)

4. Repeat steps 1 through 3 to make an additional pieced rectangle.

5. Sew the pieced rectangles together. (Figure 4)

6. Refer to the General Instructions for the Log Cabin Border (page 7), and sew the mauve strips to the outside of the square to complete the block. (Figure 5)

7. Refer to the General Instructions for Embroidery (page 8) and use the stem stitch to make the stems and leaves. (Figure 6)

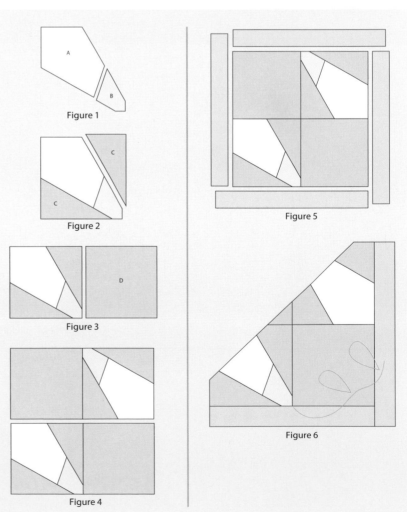

Figure 1

Figure 2

Figure 3

Figure 4

Figure 5

Figure 6

Block sizes

6" square or 8" square

Templates on page 88; enlarge 200%

Fabrics and Materials

Rose solid, mint solid, pink print, olive mottle, and green print

Coordinating thread

Cut the Pieces

1. From the rose solid, cut one piece each from Templates A and C.

2. From the mint solid, cut two pieces each from Templates A and E, and one piece from Template D. Reverse Template D and cut one additional piece.

3. From the pink print, cut one piece from Template B.

4. From the olive mottle, cut two pieces from Template F.

5. From the green print, cut one piece from Template A.

Assemble the Block

1. Sew the rose A triangle to one mint A triangle. (Figure 1)

2. Sew one mint A triangle to the B shape. (Figure 2)

3. Sew the pieced shapes together. (Figure 3)

4. Sew the green A triangle to the C shape. (Figure 4)

5. Sew the pieced shapes together. (Figure 5)

6. Sew the D shapes to the piece created in step 5. (Figure 6)

7. Sew one E shape to one F shape. Repeat to make an additional pieced triangle. (Figure 7)

8. Sew the pieced triangles to the corners to complete the block. (Figure 8)

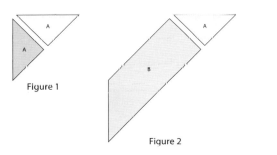

Figure 1

Figure 2

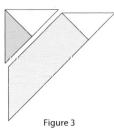

Figure 3

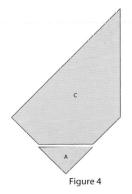

Figure 4

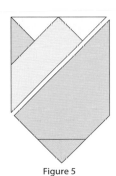

Figure 5

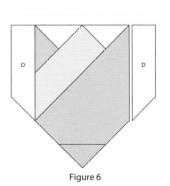

Figure 6

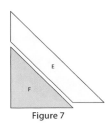

Figure 7

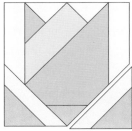

Figure 8

ORANGE COSMOS

Block sizes
6¾" square or 8½" square

Templates on page 89; enlarge 200%

Fabrics and Materials
Orange pin dot, pink solid, red solid, green solid, and teal print

Coordinating thread

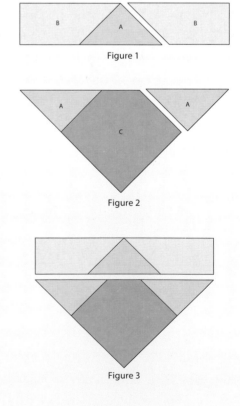

Figure 1

Figure 2

Figure 3

Cut the Pieces

1. From the orange pin dot, cut three pieces from Template A.

2. From the pink solid, cut two pieces from Template A and one piece each from Templates B, D, and E. Reverse Templates B and D and cut an additional piece from each.

3. From the red solid, cut one piece from Template C.

4. From the green solid, cut one piece from Template B. Reverse Template B and cut an additional piece.

5. From the teal print, cut one piece from Template F. (Note that the seam allowance is narrow. Because the shapes are appliquéd, the edge is turned under at the broken line.)

Assemble the Block

1. Sew two pink B shapes to one orange A triangle. (Figure 1)

2. Sew two orange A triangles to the C shape. (Figure 2)

3. Sew the pieced strip to the pieced triangle. (Figure 3)

4. Sew one pink A triangle to one green B shape. Sew one D shape to the pieced shape. Using the pieces cut when you reversed the templates, make a second pieced shape. (Figure 4)

5. Sew one pieced shape from step 4 to the pieced shape from step 3. (Figure 5)

6. Refer to the General Instructions for Hand Appliqué (page 7) and sew the F shape to the E triangles. Trim the edges. (Figure 6 & Figure 7)

7. Sew the triangle to the reverse pieced shape from step 4. (Figure 8)

8. Sew the pieced shapes together to complete the square. (Figure 9)

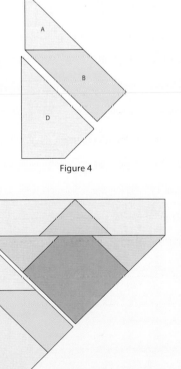

Figure 4

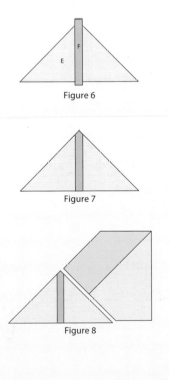

Figure 6

Figure 7

Figure 8

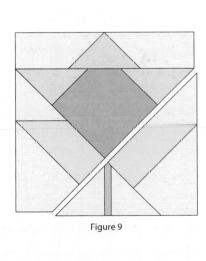

Figure 9

Figure 5

ALPINE POPPY

Block sizes
7" square or 9" square

Templates on page 89; enlarge 200%

Fabrics and Materials
Cream solid, red solid, blue print, and orange print

Coordinating thread

Cut the Pieces

1. From the cream solid, cut eight pieces from Template A and four pieces from Template D.

2. From the red solid, cut four pieces from Template B. Reverse Template B and cut four additional pieces.

3. From the blue print, cut four pieces from Template C and one piece from Template F. Reverse Template C and cut four additional pieces.

4. From the orange print, cut four pieces from Template E.

Assemble the Block

1. Sew one A triangle to one B shape. Sew one C triangle to the pieced shape. Repeat to make a total of four pieced shapes. Using the pieces cut when you reversed the templates, make four additional pieced shapes. (Figure 1)

2. Starting and stopping ¼" from the fabric edges, sew one pieced shape to one reverse pieced shape. Repeat to make a total of four pieced pairs. (Figure 2)

3. Starting and stopping ¼" from the fabric edges, sew one D square to one pieced pair. (Figure 3)

4. Align the adjoining side of the D square with the reverse shape, and starting and stopping ¼" from the fabric edges, sew the shapes together. (Figure 4)

5. Sew two pieced squares to the outsides of one E rectangle. Repeat to make a second pieced rectangle. (Figure 5)

6. Sew the remaining E rectangles to the outsides of the F square. (Figure 6)

7. Sew the pieced rectangles to the square center to complete the block. (Figure 7)

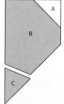

Figure 1

Figure 2

Figure 3

Figure 4

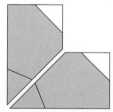

Figure 5

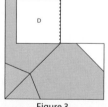

Figure 6

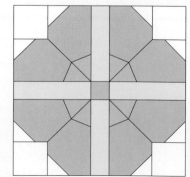

Figure 7

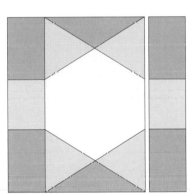

Block sizes

7" square or 8½" square

Templates on page 90; enlarge 200%

Fabrics and Materials

Brown solid, pink print, yellow solid, and lime solid

Coordinating thread

Turquoise embroidery floss

Cut the Pieces

1. From the brown solid, cut two pieces from Template A and four pieces from Template D.

2. From the pink print, cut four pieces from Template B and two pieces from Template E.

3. From the yellow solid, cut one piece from Template C.

4. From the lime solid, cut one piece from Template F. (Note that the seam allowance is narrow. Because the shapes are appliquéd, the edge is turned under at the broken line.)

Assemble the Block

1. Sew one A triangle to one B triangle. Repeat to make an additional pieced triangle. (Figure 1)

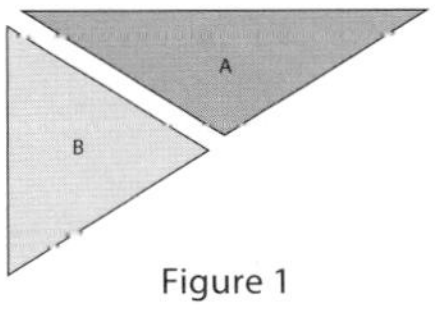

2. Sew two B triangles to the C shape. (Figure 2)

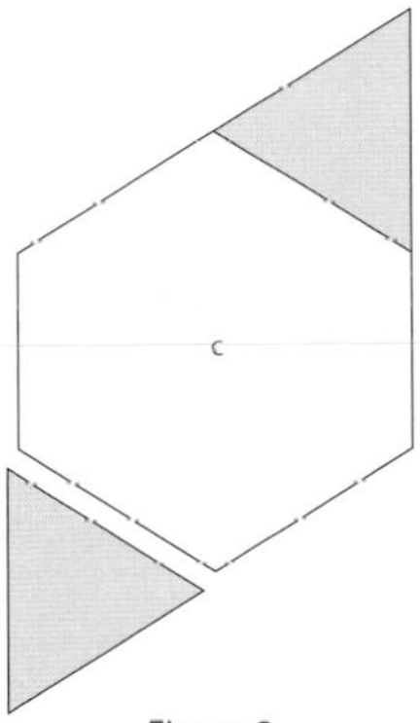

3. Sew the pieced shapes together. (Figure 3)

4. Sew two D rectangles to the ends of one E rectangle. Repeat to make a second pieced strip. (Figure 4)

5. Sew the strips to the square center to complete the block. (Figure 5)

6. Refer to the General Instructions for Hand Appliqué (page 7) and sew the F square to the flower center. (Figure 6)

7. Refer to the General Instructions for Embroidery (page 8) and use the wrapped back stitch to make the center grid. (Figure 7)

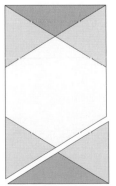

Figure 1

Figure 2

Figure 3

Figure 4

Figure 5

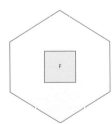

Figure 6

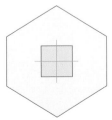

Figure 7

34 SUNFLOWER

Block sizes

7" square or 9" square

Templates on page 90; enlarge 200%

Fabrics and Materials

Yellow mottle, lavender solid, white solid, gold solid, and green solid

Coordinating thread

1 button, ¼" in diameter

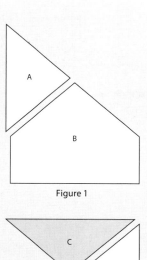

Figure 1

Figure 2

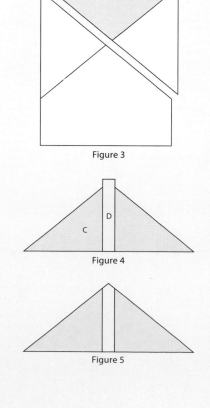

Figure 3

Figure 4

Figure 5

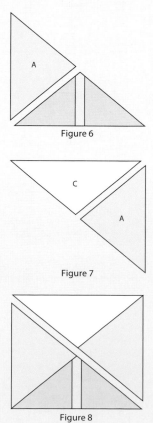

Figure 6

Figure 7

Figure 8

Cut the Pieces

1. From the yellow mottle, cut two pieces from Template A and one piece each from Templates C and E. Reverse Template E and cut an additional piece.

2. From the lavender solid, cut two pieces each from Templates C and G, and one piece from Template H. Reverse Template H and cut an additional piece.

3. From the white solid, cut one piece from Template B.

4. From the gold solid, cut one piece from Template F. Reverse Template F and cut an additional piece.

5. From the green solid, cut two pieces from Template A and one piece from Template D. (Note that the seam allowance is narrow. Because the shape is appliquéd, the edge is turned under at the broken line.)

Assemble the Block

1. Sew one yellow A triangle to the B shape. (Figure 1)

2. Sew one lavender C triangle to one yellow A triangle. (Figure 2)

3. Sew the pieced shapes together. (Figure 3)

4. Refer to the General Instructions for Hand Appliqué (page 7) and sew the D rectangle to the lavender C triangle. Trim the edges. (Figure 4 & Figure 5)

5. Sew one green A triangle to the lavender C triangle. (Figure 6)

6. Sew one yellow C triangle to one A triangle. (Figure 7)

7. Sew the pieced triangles together. (Figure 8)

8. Sew the pieced rectangles from steps 3 and 7 together. (Figure 9)

9. Sew one E shape to one F shape. (Figure 10)

10. Sew one G rectangle to the yellow mottle side of the pieced shape. Sew one H shape to the gold side of the pieced shape. (Figure 11)

11. Using the pieces cut when you reversed the templates, repeat steps 9 and 10 to make a second pieced shape.

12. Sew the pieced strips to the square center to complete the block. Sew the button to the B shape. (Figure 12)

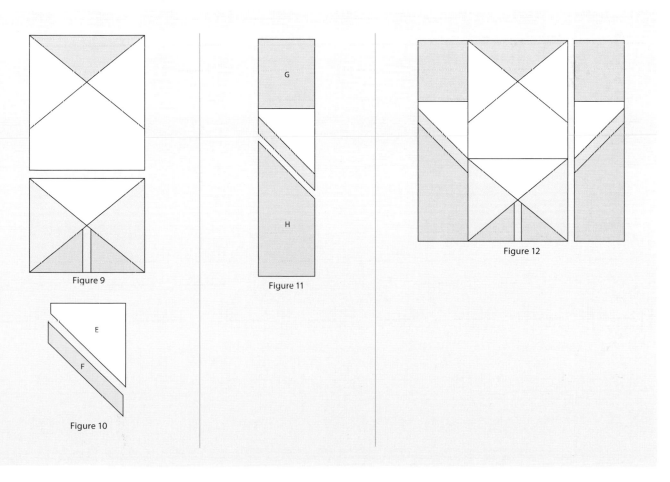

Figure 9

Figure 10

Figure 11

Figure 12

AMARYLLIS

Block sizes
7¼" square or 9" square

Templates on page 91;
enlarge 200%

Fabrics and Materials
Lime print, rose print, pink solid,
and blue solid

Coordinating thread

Yellow embroidery floss

Cut the Pieces
1. From the lime print, cut four pieces
each from Templates A and C.

2. From the rose print, cut four pieces
each from Templates B and C.

3. From the pink solid, cut one piece
from Template E.

4. From the blue solid, cut four pieces
from Template D.

Assemble the Block
1. Sew one A triangle to one B shape.
(Figure 1)

2. Sew one lime C triangle to the
pieced shape. Sew one rose C triangle
to the pieced shape. Repeat to make a
total of four pieced rectangles.
(Figure 2)

3. Sew the D triangles to the E square.
(Figure 3)

4. Refer to the General Instructions
for the Log Cabin Border (page 7)
and sew the pieced rectangles to the
square to complete the block.
(Figure 4)

5. Refer to the General Instructions for
Embroidery (page 8) and use the long
stitch to make the Xs. (Figure 5)

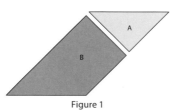

Figure 1

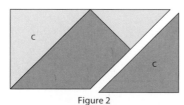

Figure 2

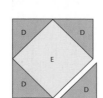

Figure 3

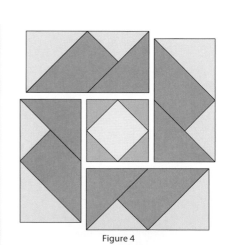

Figure 4

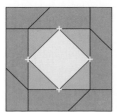

Figure 5

Block sizes

7½" square or 9" square

Templates on page 91;
enlarge 200%

Fabrics and Materials

Yellow pin dot, pink stripe,
pink print, and gray print

Coordinating thread

1 button, ½" in diameter

Cut the Pieces

1. From the yellow pin dot, cut one
piece from Template A.

2. From the pink stripe, cut one piece
each from Templates B and C.

3. From the pink print, cut four pieces
each from Templates D and F.

4. From the gray print, cut four pieces
each from Templates E, G, and H.

Assemble the Block

1. Sew the A triangle to the B shape.
Sew the C shape to the pieced shape to
create a square. (Figure 1)

2. Sew one D triangle to one E shape.
(Figure 2)

3. Sew one F shape to one G shape.
(Figure 3)

4. Sew the pieced shapes together.
(Figure 4)

5. Repeat steps 2 through 4 to make a
total of four pieced strips.

6. Sew two pieced strips to the square
center created in step 1. (Figure 5)

7. Sew two H squares to the ends of
one pieced strip. Repeat to make an
additional strip. (Figure 6)

8. Sew the strips to the square center
to complete the block. (Figure 7)

9. Sew the button to the A triangle.

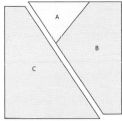

Figure 1

Figure 2

Figure 3

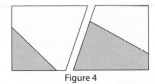

Figure 4

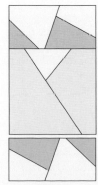

Figure 5

Figure 6

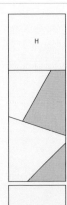

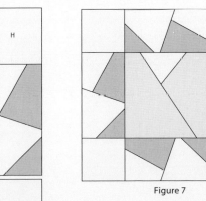

Figure 7

FORGET-ME-NOT

Block sizes
7½" square or 9" square

Templates on page 92;
enlarge 200%

Fabrics and Materials
Turquoise solid, brown print, and cream print

Coordinating thread

1 button, ½" in diameter

Cut the Pieces
1. From the turquoise solid, cut two pieces each from Templates A and E. Reverse Template E and cut two additional pieces.

2. From the brown print, cut two pieces from Template C.

3. From the cream print, cut two pieces each from Templates B, D, and F. Reverse Templates B, D, and F and cut two additional pieces from each.

Assemble the Block
1. Sew one B triangle to one A shape. Sew one reverse B triangle to the pieced shape. (Figure 1)

2. Sew one C shape to the pieced shape. (Figure 2)

3. Sew one D shape to one E shape. Sew one F shape to the pieced shape. Using the pieces cut when you reversed the templates, make an additional pieced shape. (Figure 3)

4. Sew two pieced corner shapes from step 3 to one pieced center shape. Repeat steps 1 through 4 to make a second pieced rectangle. (Figure 4)

5. Sew the rectangles together to complete the block. Sew the button to the flower center. (Figure 5)

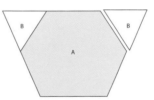

Figure 1

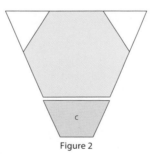

Figure 2

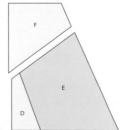

Figure 3

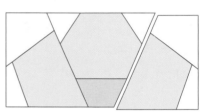

Figure 4

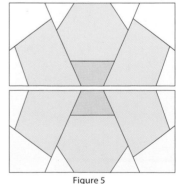

Figure 5

Block sizes
6½" square or 8" square

Templates on page 92; enlarge 200%

Fabrics and Materials
Cream solid, blue solid, blue print, and green solid

Coordinating thread

Green embroidery floss

Cut the Pieces

1. From the cream solid, cut four pieces from Template A, one piece from Template B, and three pieces from Template D.

2. From the blue solid, cut one piece from Template A and two pieces from Template C. Reverse Template C and cut an additional piece.

3. From the blue print, cut one piece from Template B.

4. From the green solid, cut two pieces from Template A.

Assemble the Block

1. Sew the blue A triangle to one cream A triangle. Sew the cream B square to the pieced square. (Figure 1)

2. Sew one cream A triangle to one C shape. (Figure 2)

3. Sew the pieced rectangles together. (Figure 3)

4. Sew one A triangle to one C shape. Using the piece cut when you reversed template C, make a second pieced shape. (Figure 4)

5. Sew one pieced triangle to the pieced square. (Figure 5)

6. Sew the green A triangles to the blue B square. (Figure 6)

7. Sew the pieced triangles from steps 4 and 6 together to create a larger triangle. (Figure 7)

8. Sew the large pieced triangle to the pieced shape. (Figure 8)

9. Sew the D triangles to the piece created in step 8 to complete the block. (Figure 9)

10. Refer to the General Instructions for Embroidery (page 8) and use the chain stitch to make the stem. (Figure 10)

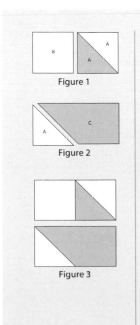

Figure 1

Figure 2

Figure 3

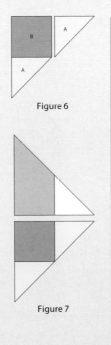

Figure 4

Figure 5

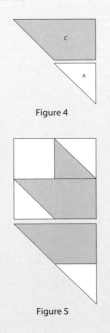

Figure 6

Figure 7

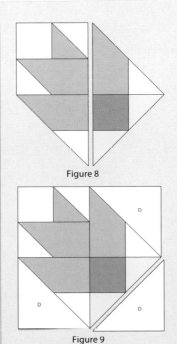

Figure 8

Figure 9

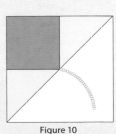

Figure 10

39
JASMINE

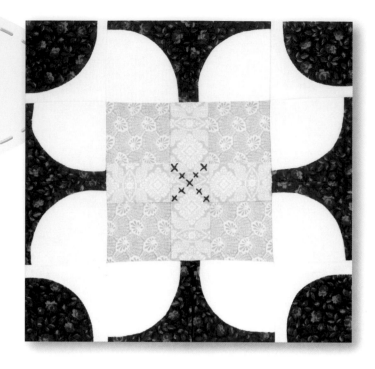

Block sizes
8" square or 9½" square

Templates on page 93; enlarge 200%

Fabrics and Materials
Gold print, light blue print, dark blue print, and white solid

Coordinating thread

Navy embroidery floss

Cut the Pieces
1. From the gold print, cut four pieces from Template A.

2. From the light blue print, cut two pieces from Template B and one piece from Template C.

3. From the dark blue print, cut eight pieces from Template D and four pieces from Template E.

4. From the white solid, cut four pieces from Template D and eight pieces from Template E.

Assemble the Block
1. Sew two A squares to one B rectangle. Repeat to make an additional pieced rectangle. (Figure 1)

2. Sew the pieced rectangles to the C strip. (Figure 2)

3. Refer to the General Instructions for Curve Patch Piecing (page 8) and sew one blue D shape to one white E shape. Repeat to make a total of eight pieced squares. (Figure 3)

4. Sew two pieced squares together. Repeat to make a total of four pieced rectangles. (Figure 4)

5. Sew two pieced rectangles to the square center. (Figure 5)

6. Sew one white D shape to one blue E shape. Repeat to make a total of four pieced squares. (Figure 6)

7. Sew two pieced squares from step 6 to one pieced rectangle from step 4. Repeat to make an additional pieced strip. (Figure 7)

8. Sew the pieced strips to the square center to complete the block. (Figure 8)

9. Refer to the General Instructions for Embroidery (page 8) and use the cross stitch to make the center X. (Figure 9)

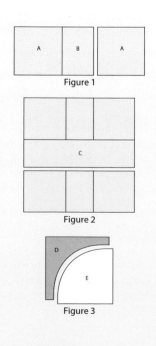

Figure 1

Figure 2

Figure 3

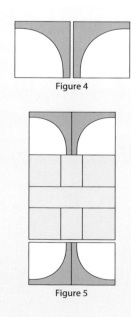

Figure 4

Figure 5

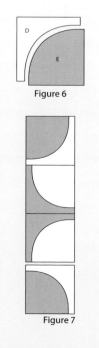

Figure 6

Figure 7

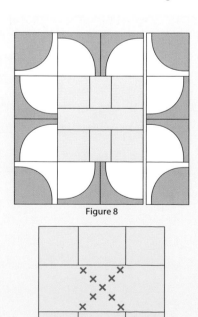

Figure 8

Figure 9

Block sizes

6½" square or 8" square

Templates on page 93; enlarge 200%

Fabrics and Materials

Pink solid, melon solid, blue pin stripe, olive print, and periwinkle solid

Coordinating thread

Orange embroidery floss

Cut the Pieces

1. From the pink solid, cut two pieces from Template A.

2. From the melon solid, cut two pieces from Template A.

3. From the blue pin stripe, cut three pieces from Template B.

4. From the olive print, cut three pieces from Template B.

5. From the periwinkle solid, cut two pieces each from Templates B and D, and one piece from Template C. Reverse Template C and cut an additional piece.

Assemble the Block

1. Sew one pink A shape to the green B triangle. Sew the remaining A shapes to the blue B triangles. (Figure 1)

2. Sew the pieced shapes together to create a square. (Figure 2)

3. Sew one periwinkle B triangle to one olive B triangle. Sew one C shape to the pieced triangle. Using the piece cut when you reversed the template, make a second pieced shape. (Figure 3)

4. Sew the pieced triangles and the D triangles to the square center to complete the block. (Figure 4)

5. Refer to the General Instructions for Embroidery (page 8) and use the long stitch and French Knot to make the flower detail. (Figure 5)

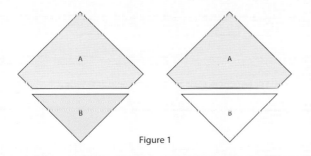

Figure 1

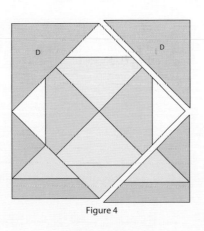

Figure 2

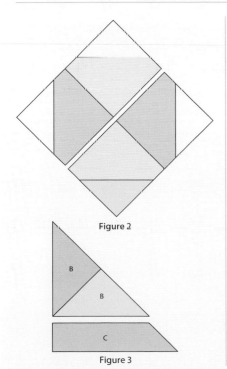

Figure 3

Figure 4

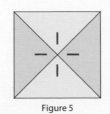

Figure 5

41
AUTUMN PANSY

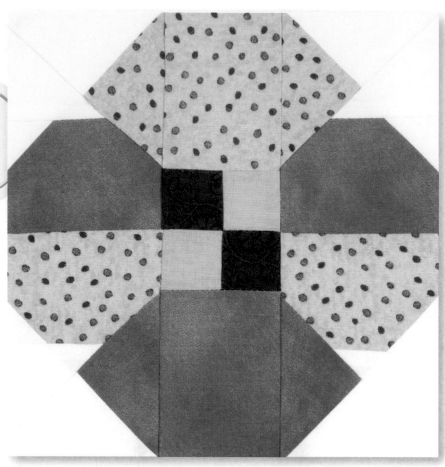

Block sizes

7½" square or 9" square

Templates on page 93; enlarge 200%

Fabrics and Materials

Lavender solid, violet print, gold print, rust mottle, and white solid

Coordinating thread

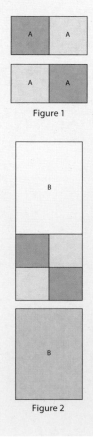

Figure 1

Figure 2

Cut the Pieces

1. From the lavender solid, cut two pieces from Template A.

2. From the violet print, cut two pieces from Template A.

3. From the gold print, cut one piece each from Templates B and C, and two pieces from Template E. Reverse Template C and cut an additional piece.

4. From the rust mottle, cut one piece each from Templates B and C, and two pieces from Template E. Reverse Template C and cut an additional piece.

5. From the white solid, cut eight pieces from Template E and four pieces from Template D.

Assemble the Block

1. Sew the A squares together to create a larger square. (Figure 1)

2. Sew the B rectangles to the ends of the pieced square. (Figure 2)

3. Sew one D triangle to one rust C shape. Repeat with the reverse rust C shape. (Figure 3)

4. Repeat step 3 with the D triangles and the gold C shapes.

5. Sew one white E triangle to one rust pieced shape. Repeat with the reverse shape. (Figure 4)

6. Repeat step 5 with the white E triangles and the gold shapes.

7. Sew one white E triangle to one gold E triangle. Repeat with the remaining gold and rust E triangles. (Figure 5)

8. Sew one pieced triangle to one pieced shape created in step 5. Repeat with the remaining pieced triangles and pieced shapes. (Figure 6)

9. Sew one pieced shape to one reverse pieced shape of opposite color. Repeat with the remaining pieced shapes. (Figure 7)

10. Sew the pieced rectangles to the center strip to complete the block. (Figure 8)

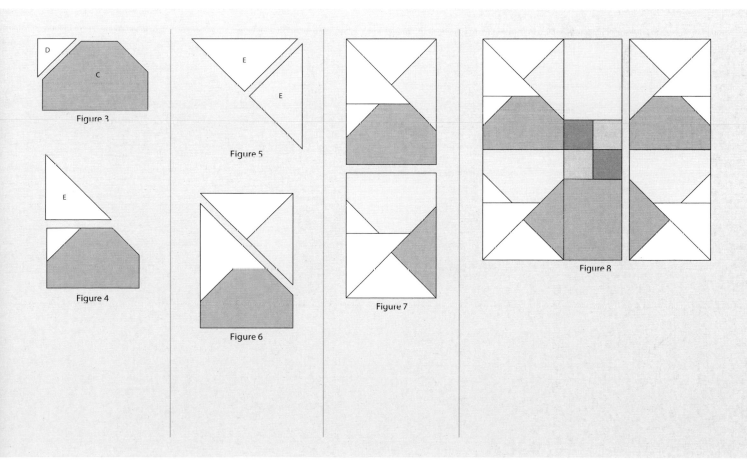

Figure 3

Figure 4

Figure 5

Figure 6

Figure 7

Figure 8

PAPER WHITE

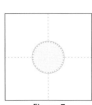
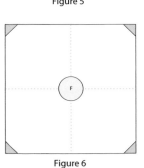
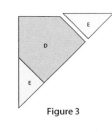
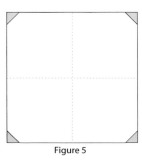

Block sizes

7¼" square or 9" square

Templates on page 94; enlarge 200%

Fabrics and Materials

Navy solid, white solid, blue print, turquoise solid, and yellow solid

Coordinating thread

Yellow embroidery floss

1 button, ¼" in diameter

Cut the Pieces

1. From the navy solid, cut four pieces from Template A.

2. From the white solid, cut four pieces from Template B and one piece from Template C.

3. From the blue print, cut four pieces from Template D.

4. From the turquoise solid, cut eight pieces from Template E.

5. From the yellow solid, cut one piece from Template F. (Note that the seam allowance is narrow. Because the shapes are appliquéd, the edge is turned under at the broken line.)

Assemble the Block

1. Sew one A shape to one B triangle. Repeat to make a total of four pieced triangles. (Figure 1)

2. Sew the pieced triangles to the C shape. (Figure 2)

3. Sew two E triangles to one D shape. Repeat to make a total of four pieced triangles. (Figure 3)

4. Sew the pieced triangles to the square center to complete the block. (Figure 4)

5. Refer to the General Instructions for Embroidery (page 8) and use the running stitch to make the center grid. (Figure 5)

6. Refer to the General Instructions for Hand Appliqué (page 7) and sew the F circle to the flower center. (Figure 6)

7. Use the blanket stitch to outline the circle. Sew the button to the circle. (Figure 7)

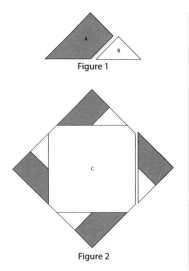

Figure 1

Figure 2

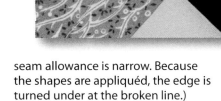

Figure 3

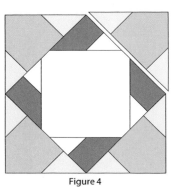

Figure 4

Figure 5

Figure 6

Figure 7

CROCUS

Block sizes

7¼" square or 9" square

Templates on page 94; enlarge 200%

Fabrics and Materials

White solid, gold print, turquoise print, and purple solid

Coordinating thread

Brown embroidery floss

Cut the Pieces

1. From the white solid, cut one piece from Template A.

2. From the gold print, cut two pieces from Template B, and one piece each from Templates C and E. Reverse Template E and cut an additional piece.

3. From the turquoise print, cut two pieces from Template D, four pieces from Template H, and one piece from Template F. Reverse Template F and cut an additional piece.

4. From the purple solid, cut four pieces from Template G.

Assemble the Block

1. Sew the B triangles to the A shape. (Figure 1)

2. Sew the pieced rectangle to the C shape. (Figure 2)

3. Sew one D rectangle to one E shape. Sew one D rectangle to the reverse E shape. (Figure 3)

4. Sew the pieced shapes to the piece created in step 2. (Figure 4)

5. Sew the F triangles to the pieced shape to create a square. (Figure 5)

6. Sew two G strips to the square center. (Figure 6)

7. Sew two H squares to the ends of each remaining G strip. (Figure 7)

8. Sew the pieced strips to the center rectangle to complete the block. (Figure 8)

9. Refer to the General Instructions for Embroidery (page 8) and use the running stitch and the French knot to make the stamen. (Figure 9)

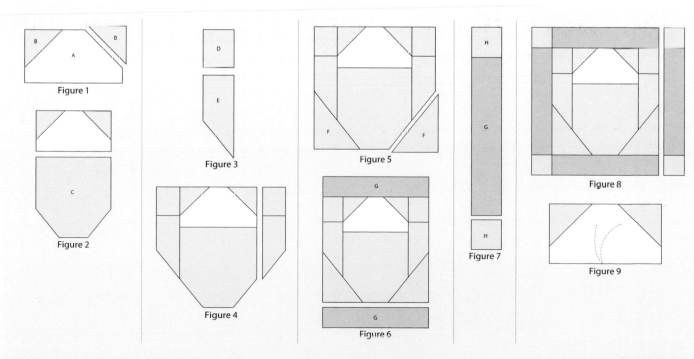

Figure 1

Figure 2

Figure 3

Figure 4

Figure 5

Figure 6

Figure 7

Figure 8

Figure 9

GERBER DAISY

Block sizes

6" x 8¼" rectangle or
7½" x 10¼" rectangle

Templates on page 95;
enlarge 200%

Fabrics and Materials

Pink solid, white solid, red solid,
orange pin dot, and green solid

Coordinating thread

Green embroidery floss

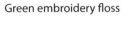

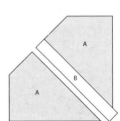

Figure 1

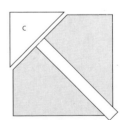

Figure 2

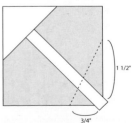

Figure 3

Cut the Pieces

1. From the pink solid, cut four pieces from Template A. Reverse Template A and cut four additional pieces.

2. From the white solid, cut four pieces each from Templates B and C, and one piece each from Templates F, G, and H. Reverse Template H and cut an additional piece.

3. From the red solid, cut four pieces from Template D.

4. From the orange pin dot, reverse Template D and cut four pieces.

5. From the green solid, cut one piece from Template E. Reverse Template E and cut an additional piece.

Assemble the Block

1. Sew two A shapes to one B strip. (Figure 1)

2. Sew one C triangle to the pieced shape. (Figure 2)

3. Mark and trim the square. (Figure 3 & Figure 4)

4. Sew one red triangle to the trimmed shape. (Figure 5)

5. Mark and trim the square. (Figure 6 & Figure 7)

6. Sew one orange D triangle to the trimmed shape. (Figure 8)

7. Repeat steps 1 through 6 to make four pieced squares.

8. Sew the pieced squares together. (Figure 9)

9. Sew one E shape to the F triangle. (Figure 10)

10. Sew one E shape to the G triangle. (Figure 11)

11. Sew the pieced shapes together. (Figure 12)

12. Sew the H shapes to the pieced shape. (Figure 13)

13. Sew the pieced rectangle to the square center to complete the block. (Figure 14)

14. Refer to the General Instructions for Embroidery (page 8) and use three rows of running stitches to make the stem. (Figure 15)

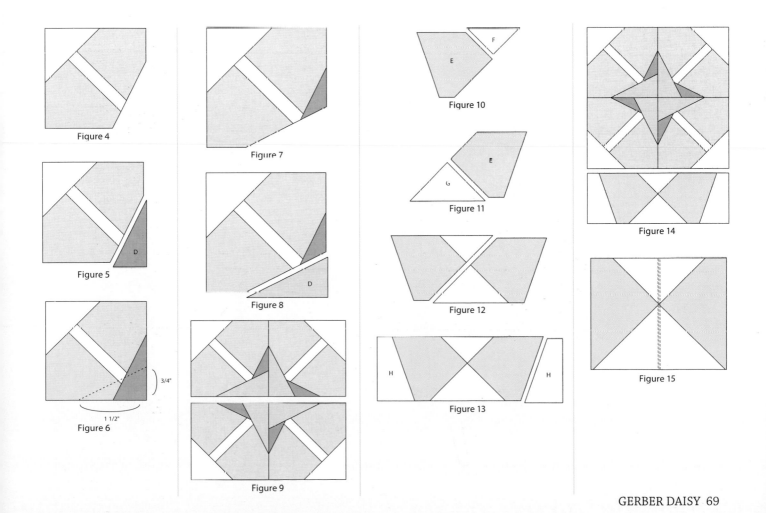

Figure 4

Figure 5

Figure 6

1 1/2"

3/4"

Figure 7

Figure 8

Figure 9

Figure 10

Figure 11

Figure 12

Figure 13

Figure 14

Figure 15

LADY'S SLIPPER

Block sizes
7½" square or 9" square

Templates on page 95; enlarge 200%

Fabrics and Materials
Cream mottle, melon solid, gold print, pink print, and green print

Coordinating thread

Green embroidery floss

Cut the Pieces
1. From the cream mottle, cut two pieces each from Templates A, B, and D, and one piece each from Templates F and H. Reverse Template H and cut an additional piece.

2. From the melon solid, cut two pieces from Template C and one piece from Template E.

3. From the gold print, cut four pieces from Template A.

4. From the pink print, cut one piece from Template D.

5. From the green print, cut one piece from Template G. Reverse Template G and cut an additional piece.

Assemble the Block
1. Sew one gold A triangle to one B square. (Figure 1)

2. Sew one gold A triangle to one C shape. (Figure 2)

3. Sew the pieced shapes together. (Figure 3)

4. Sew two A triangles to the E shape to create a larger triangle. (Figure 4)

5. Sew one cream D triangle to the pieced shape created in step 3. (Figure 5)

6. Repeat steps 1, 2, 3, and 5 to make another pieced shape that is the reverse of the piece completed in step 5.

7. Sew the piece created in step 5 to the triangle created in step 4. (Figure 6)

8. Starting and stopping ¼" from the fabric edges, sew one G shape to the F triangle. (Figure 7)

9. Starting and stopping ¼" from the fabric edges, sew the reverse G shape to the adjoining side of the F triangle. (Figure 8)

10. Align the G shapes, and starting and stopping ¼" from the fabric edges, sew the G shapes together. (Figure 9)

11. Sew the pink D triangle to the pieced shape created in step 10 to make a square. (Figure 10)

12. Sew the H shapes to the pieced square created in step 11. (Figure 11)

13. Sew the pieced shape completed in step 12 to the reverse piece created in step 6. (Figure 12)

14. Sew the pieced shape to the triangle created in step 7 to complete the block. (Figure 13)

15. Refer to the General Instructions for Embroidery (page 8) and use the cross stitch to make the stem. (Figure 14)

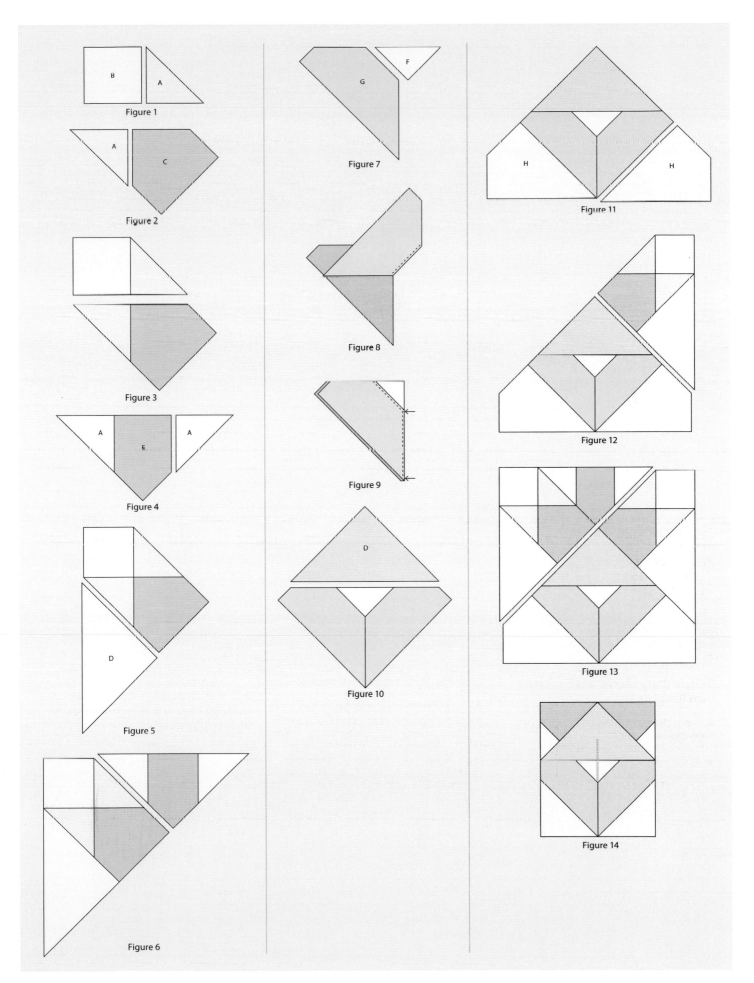

Figure 1

Figure 2

Figure 3

Figure 4

Figure 5

Figure 6

Figure 7

Figure 8

Figure 9

Figure 10

Figure 11

Figure 12

Figure 13

Figure 14

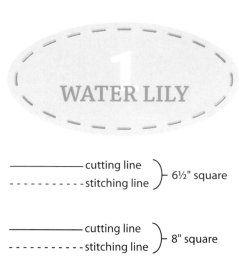

WATER LILY

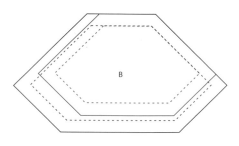

——————— cutting line
- - - - - - - stitching line } 6½" square

——————— cutting line
- - - - - - - stitching line } 8" square

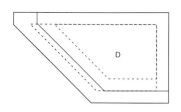

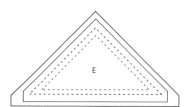

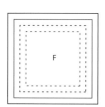

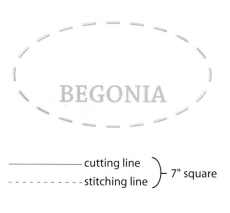

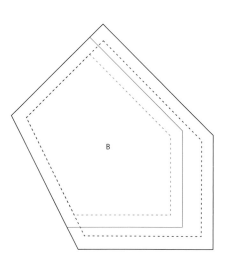

BEGONIA

——————— cutting line
- - - - - - - stitching line } 7" square

——————— cutting line
- - - - - - - stitching line } 8½" square

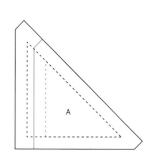

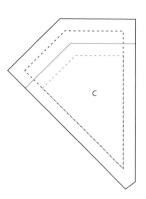

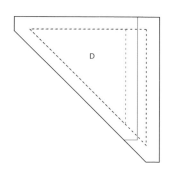

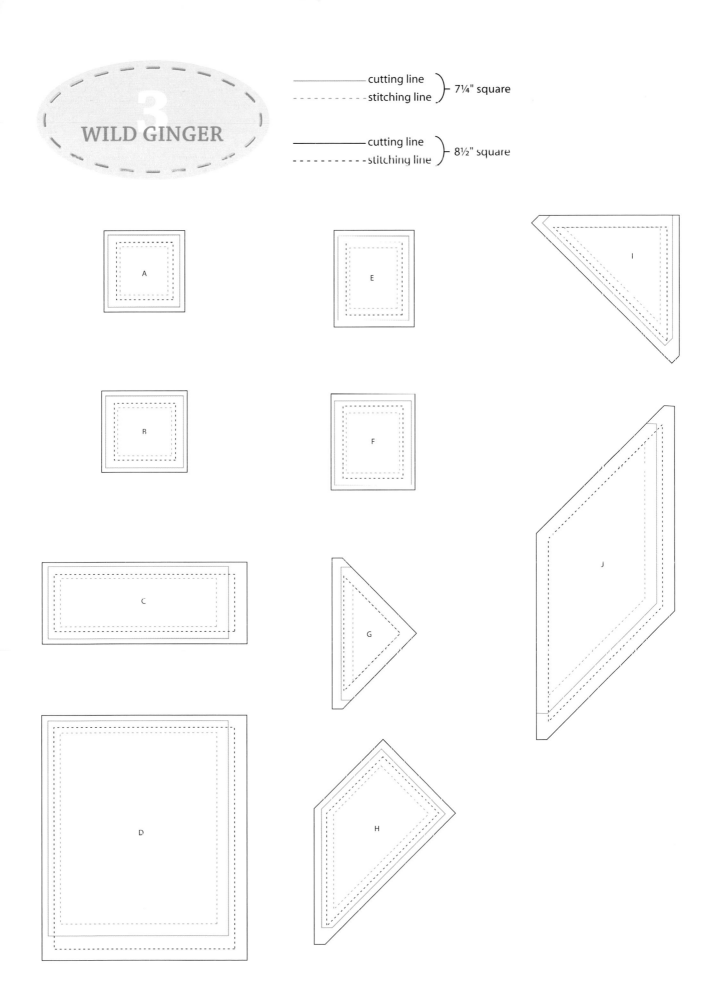

WILD GINGER

3

———— cutting line
- - - - - stitching line
} 7¼" square

———— cutting line
- - - - - stitching line
} 8½" square

A

E

I

B

F

J

C

G

D

H

SUMMER BOUQUET

A

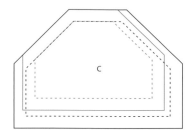

C

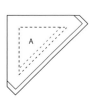

B

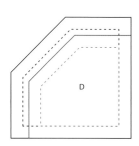

D

SUNRISE DAYLILY

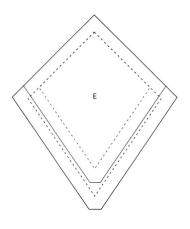

E

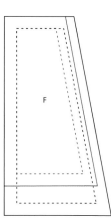

F

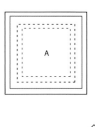

A

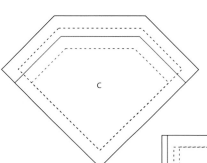

C

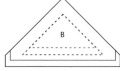

B

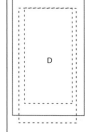

D

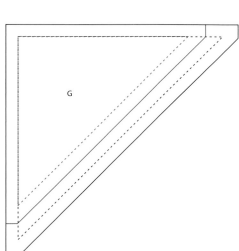

G

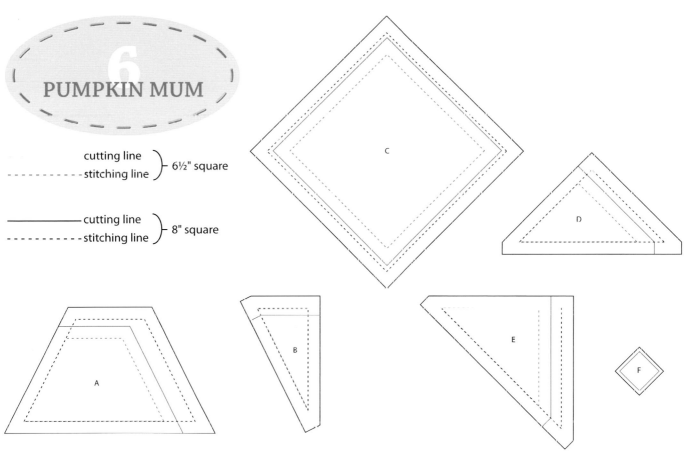

PUMPKIN MUM

cutting line
— — — stitching line ⎱ 6½" square

——————— cutting line
– – – – – stitching line ⎱ 8" square

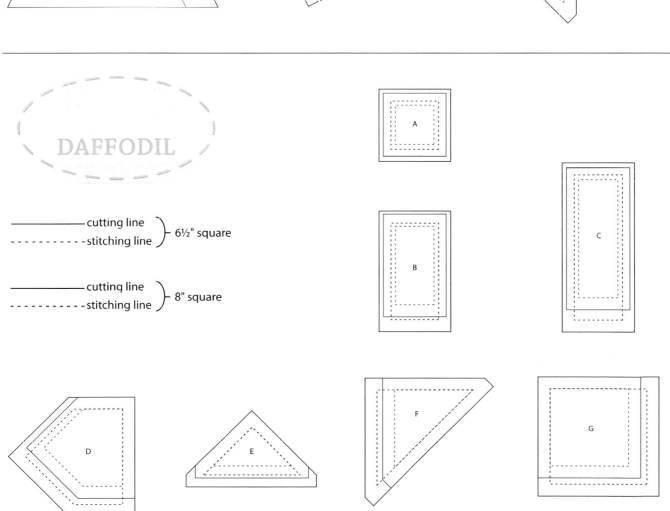

DAFFODIL

——————— cutting line
– – – – – stitching line ⎱ 6½" square

——————— cutting line
– – – – – stitching line ⎱ 8" square

ROSE CORSAGE

cutting line
stitching line } 7" square

cutting line
stitching line } 8½" square

A

B

C

D

E

F

G

FLAME AZALEA

cutting line
stitching line } 7½" square

cutting line
stitching line } 8¾" square

A

B

C

D

E

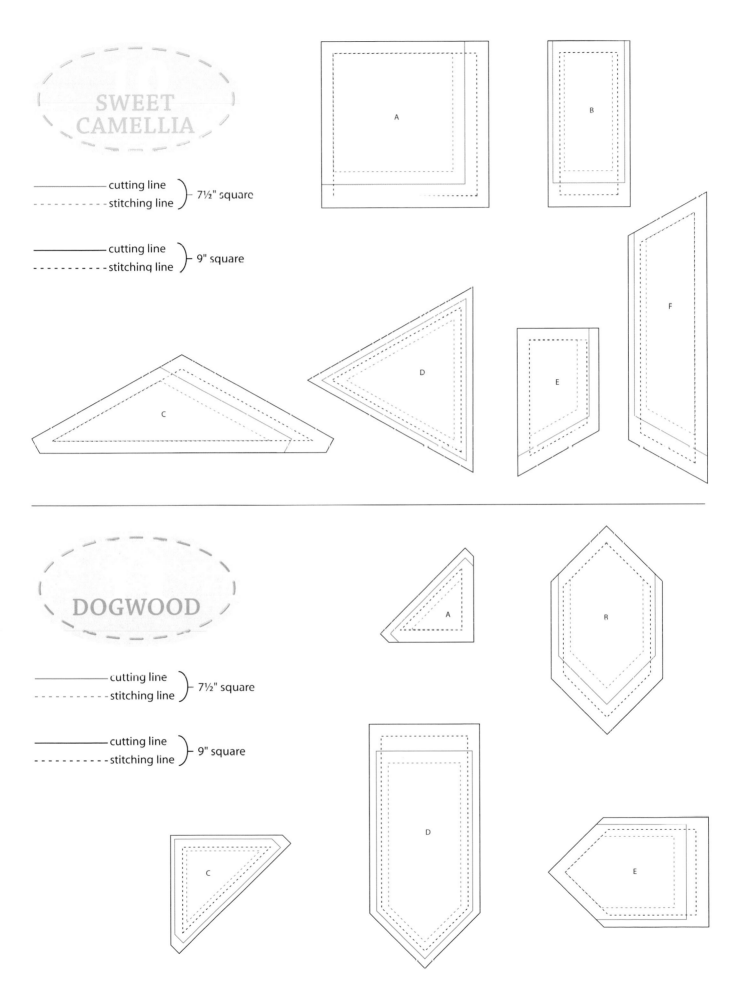

SWEET CAMELLIA

cutting line
stitching line ⎞ 7½" square

cutting line
stitching line ⎞ 9" square

A

B

C

D

E

F

DOGWOOD

cutting line
stitching line ⎞ 7½" square

cutting line
stitching line ⎞ 9" square

A

B

C

D

E

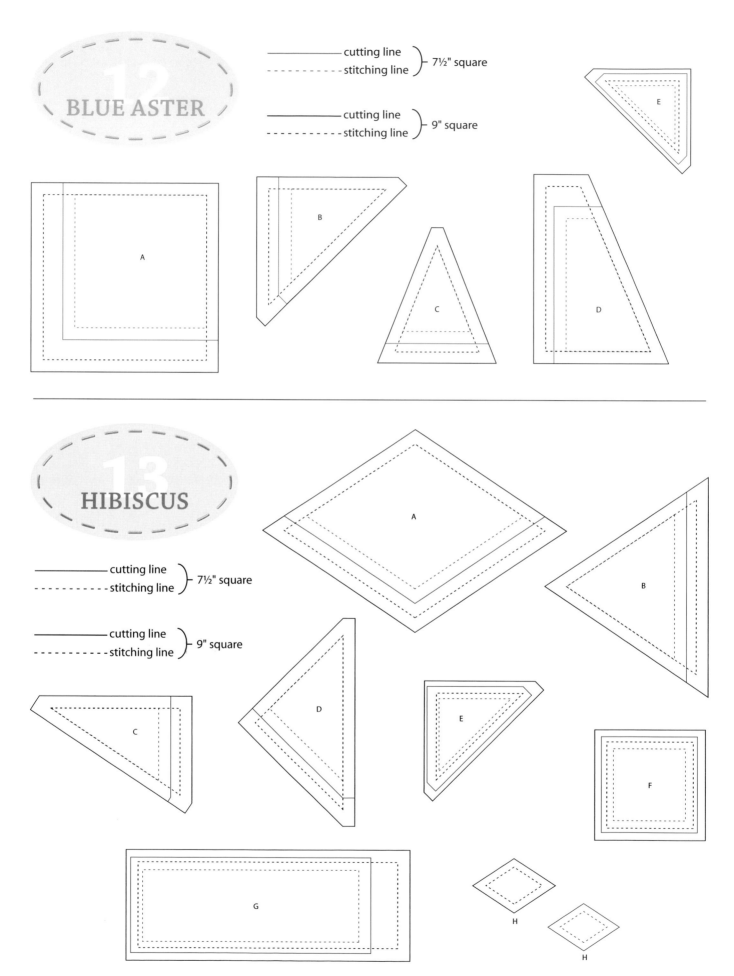

12 BLUE ASTER

cutting line
stitching line } 7½" square

cutting line
stitching line } 9" square

A

B

C

D

E

13 HIBISCUS

cutting line
stitching line } 7½" square

cutting line
stitching line } 9" square

A

B

C

D

E

F

G

H

H

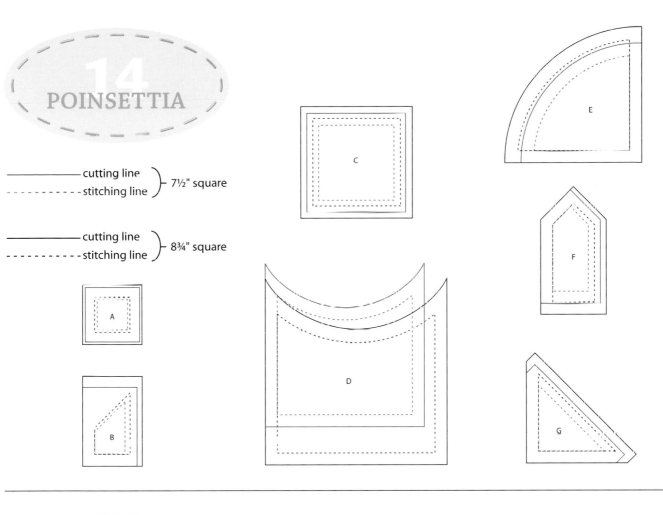

14 POINSETTIA

cutting line
stitching line } 7½" square

cutting line
stitching line } 8¾" square

C

E

F

A

B

D

G

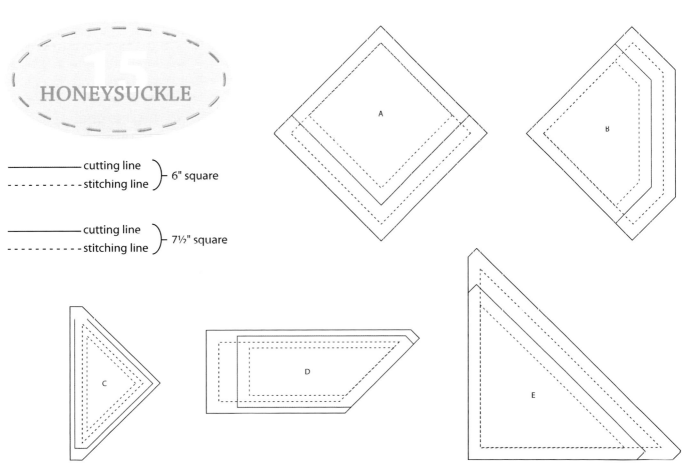

15 HONEYSUCKLE

cutting line
stitching line } 6" square

cutting line
stitching line } 7½" square

A

B

C

D

E

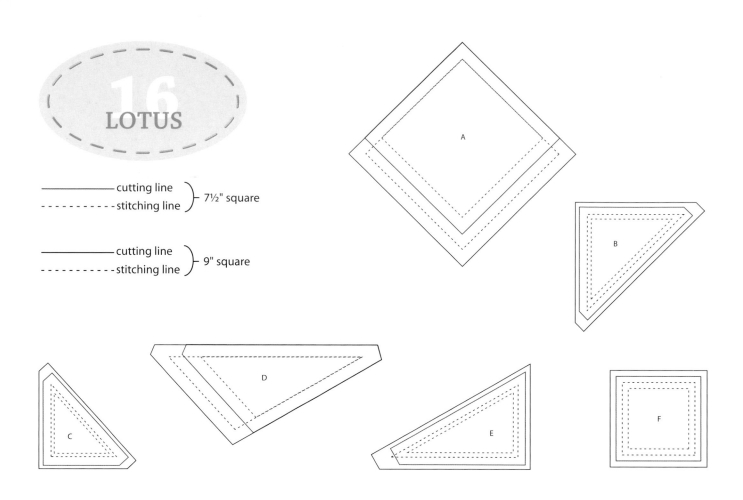

16 LOTUS

—————— cutting line ⎤
- - - - - - stitching line ⎦ 7½" square

—————— cutting line ⎤
- - - - - - stitching line ⎦ 9" square

A

B

C

D

E

F

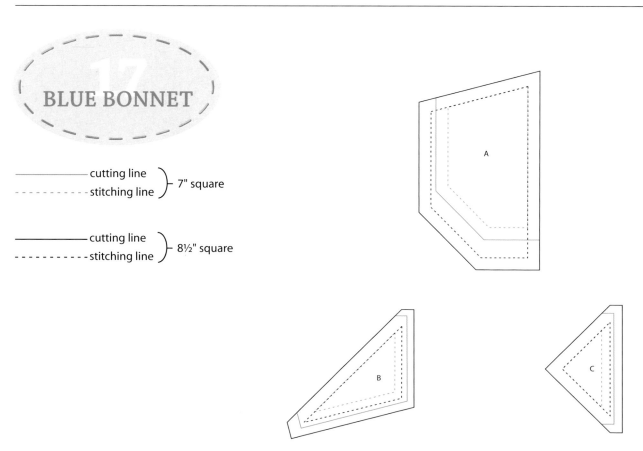

17 BLUE BONNET

—————— cutting line ⎤
- - - - - - stitching line ⎦ 7" square

—————— cutting line ⎤
- - - - - - stitching line ⎦ 8½" square

A

B

C

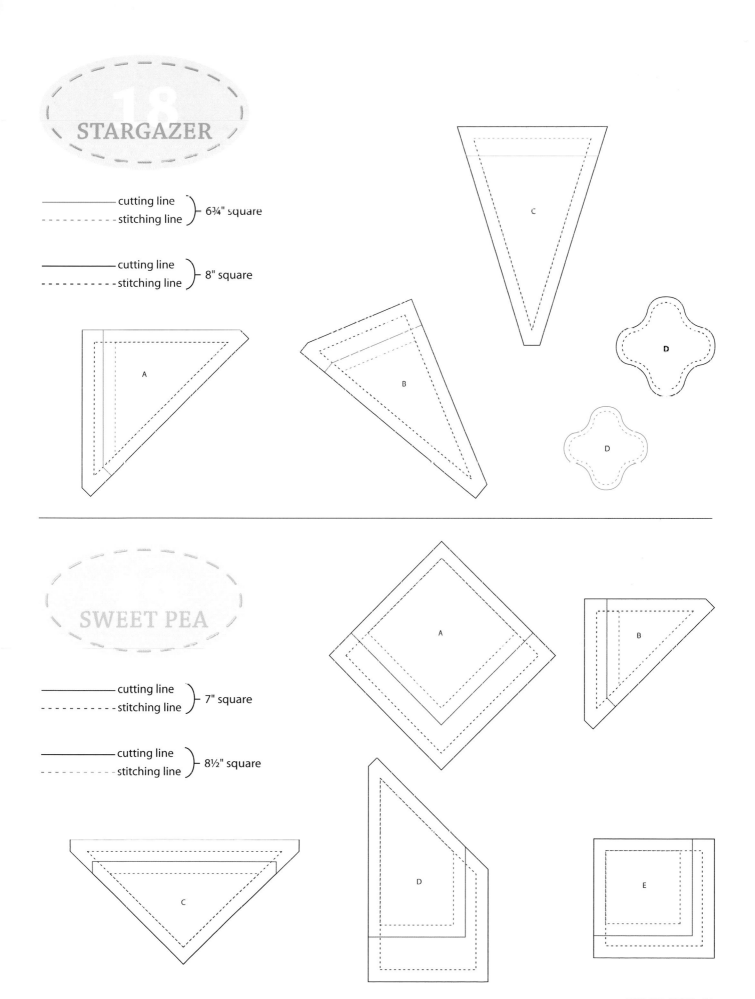

18 STARGAZER

cutting line
stitching line ⟩ 6¾" square

cutting line
stitching line ⟩ 8" square

A

B

C

D

D

SWEET PEA

cutting line
stitching line ⟩ 7" square

cutting line
stitching line ⟩ 8½" square

A

B

C

D

E

20 ROSE OF SHARON

——— cutting line
- - - - - stitching line ⎬ 5" x 8" rectangle

——— cutting line
- - - - - stitching line ⎬ 6¼" x 10" rectangle

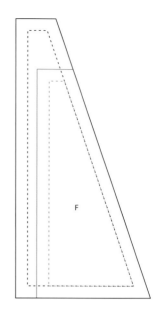

F

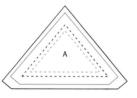

A

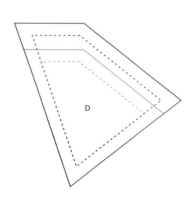

D

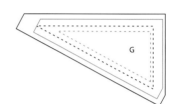

G

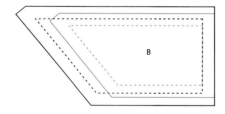

B

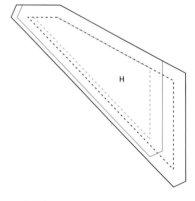

H

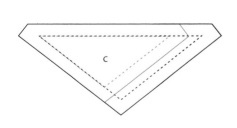

C

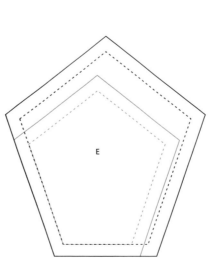

E

I

PHLOX

21

—————— cutting line
- - - - - - - stitching line } 7" square

—————— cutting line
- - - - - - - stitching line } 9" square

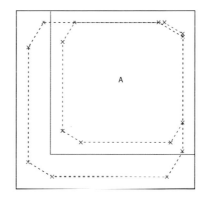

A

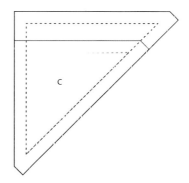

C

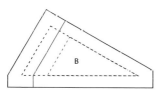

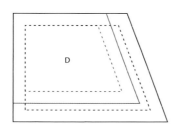

B

D

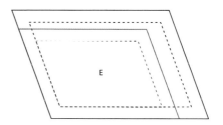

E

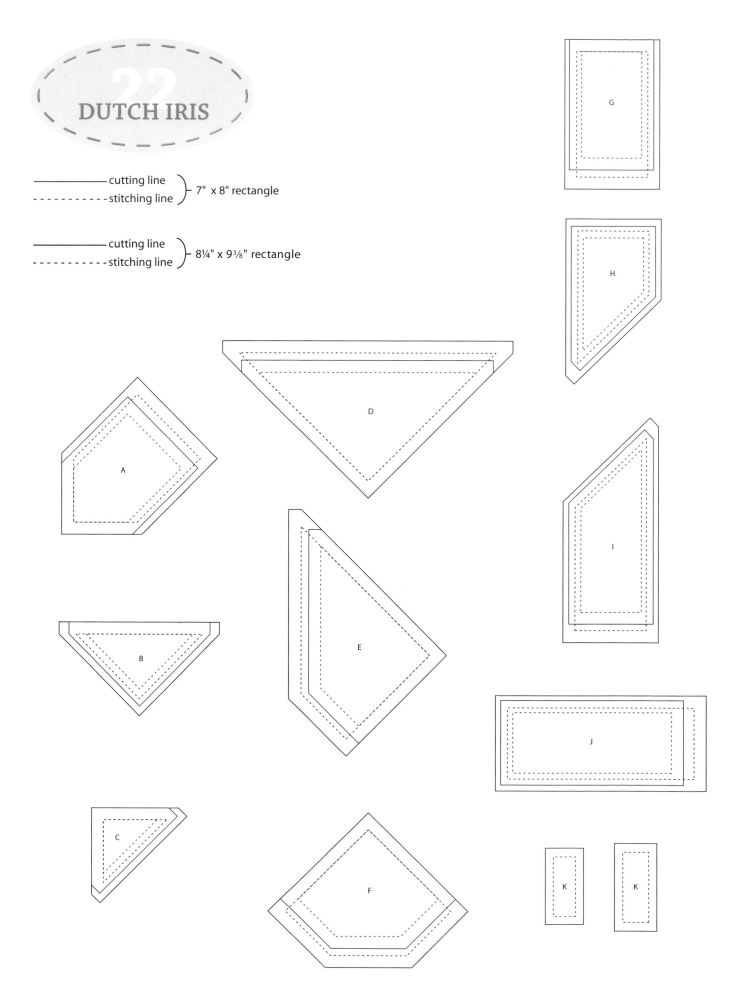

DUTCH IRIS

— cutting line ⎫
---- stitching line ⎬ 7" x 8" rectangle

— cutting line ⎫
---- stitching line ⎬ 8¼" x 9⅜" rectangle

G

H

D

A

I

B

E

J

C

F

K   K

ANEMONE

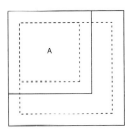

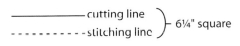

———— cutting line
- - - - - - stitching line $\Big\}$ 6¼" square

———— cutting line
- - - - - - stitching line $\Big\}$ 7¾" square

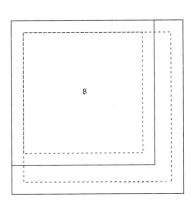

———

GARDEN TRELLIS

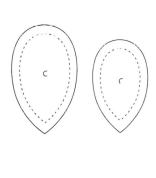

———— cutting line
- - - - - - stitching line $\Big\}$ 8" square

———— cutting line
- - - - - - stitching line $\Big\}$ 9½" square

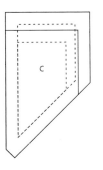

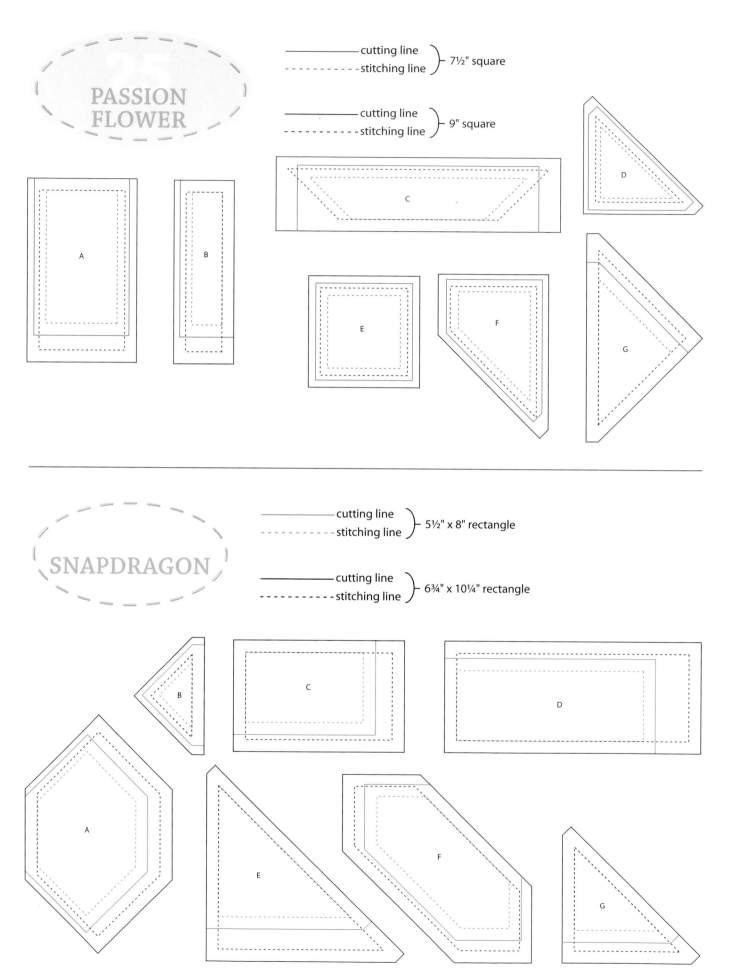

PASSION
FLOWER

cutting line
stitching line $\}$ 7½" square

cutting line
stitching line $\}$ 9" square

A

B

C

D

E

F

G

SNAPDRAGON

cutting line
stitching line $\}$ 5½" x 8" rectangle

cutting line
stitching line $\}$ 6¾" x 10¼" rectangle

A

B

C

D

E

F

G

GHOST ORCHID

27

cutting line ⎫
stitching line ⎭ 7" square

cutting line ⎫
stitching line ⎭ 9" square

A

B

C

D

E

F

G

HOLLYHOCK

cutting line ⎫
stitching line ⎭ 7" square

cutting line ⎫
stitching line ⎭ 8½" square

A

B

C

D

E

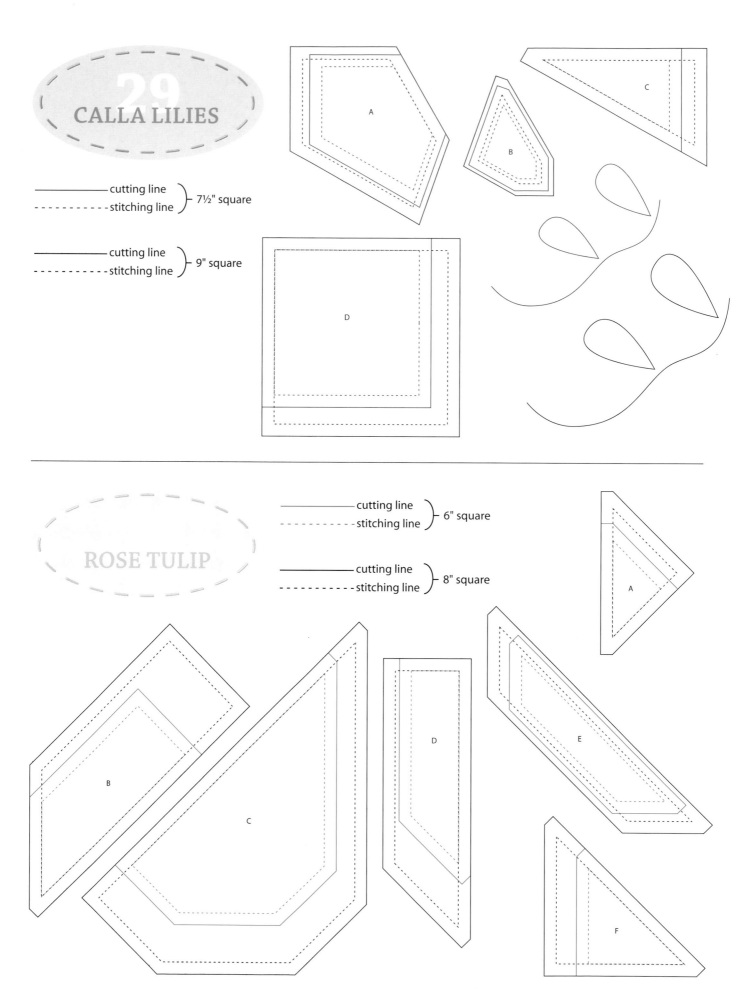

29
CALLA LILIES

——— cutting line
– – – – stitching line $\Big\}$ 7½" square

——— cutting line
– – – – stitching line $\Big\}$ 9" square

A

B

C

D

ROSE TULIP

——— cutting line
– – – – stitching line $\Big\}$ 6" square

——— cutting line
– – – – stitching line $\Big\}$ 8" square

A

B

C

D

E

F

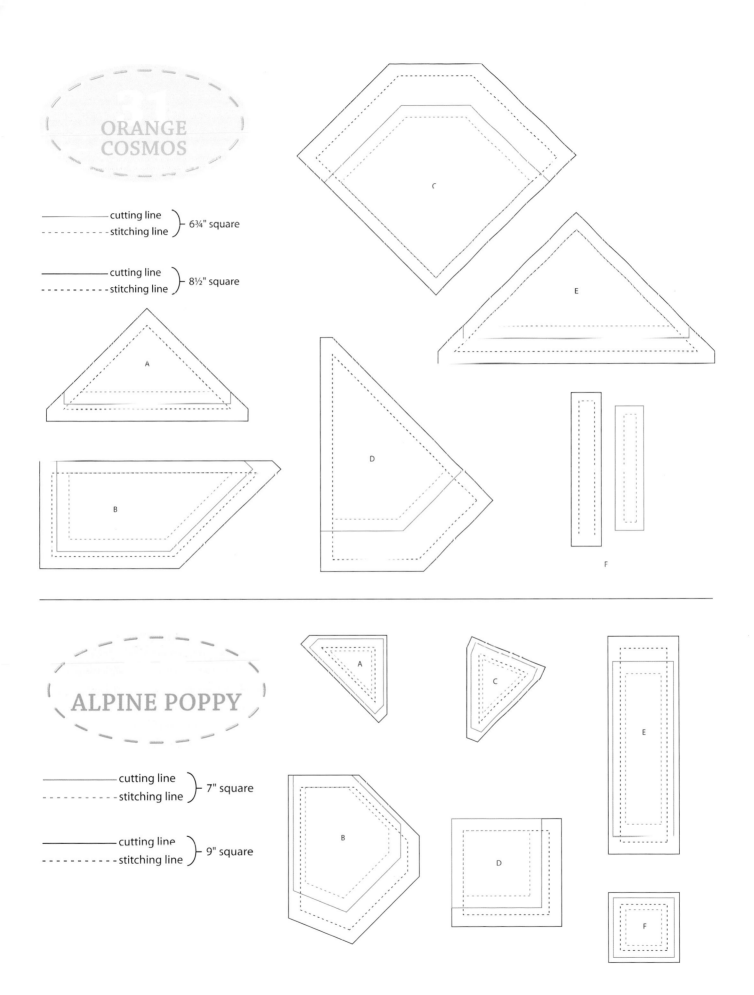

ORANGE COSMOS

cutting line ⎫
stitching line ⎭ 6¾" square

cutting line ⎫
stitching line ⎭ 8½" square

A

B

C

D

E

F

ALPINE POPPY

cutting line ⎫
stitching line ⎭ 7" square

cutting line ⎫
stitching line ⎭ 9" square

A

B

C

D

E

F

FUCHSIA

—————— cutting line
- - - - - - stitching line ⎫ 7" square

—————— cutting line
- - - - - - stitching line ⎫ 8½" square

A

B

C

D

E

F

SUNFLOWER

—————— cutting line
- - - - - - stitching line ⎫ 7" square

—————— cutting line
- - - - - - stitching line ⎫ 9" square

C

D

E

F

G

H

A

B

AMARYLLIS

——— cutting line
- - - - - stitching line } 7¼" square

——— cutting line
- - - - - stitching line } 9" square

A

B

C

D

E

MORNING GLORY

——— cutting line
- - - - - stitching line } 7½" square

——— cutting line
- - - - - stitching line } 9" square

A

B

C

D

E

F

G

H

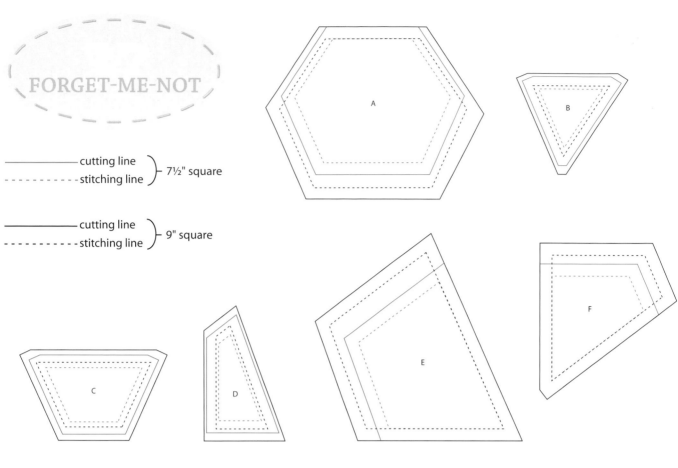

FORGET-ME-NOT

⎯⎯⎯⎯ cutting line
- - - - - - - stitching line ⎬ 7½" square

⎯⎯⎯⎯ cutting line
- - - - - - - stitching line ⎬ 9" square

A

B

C

D

E

F

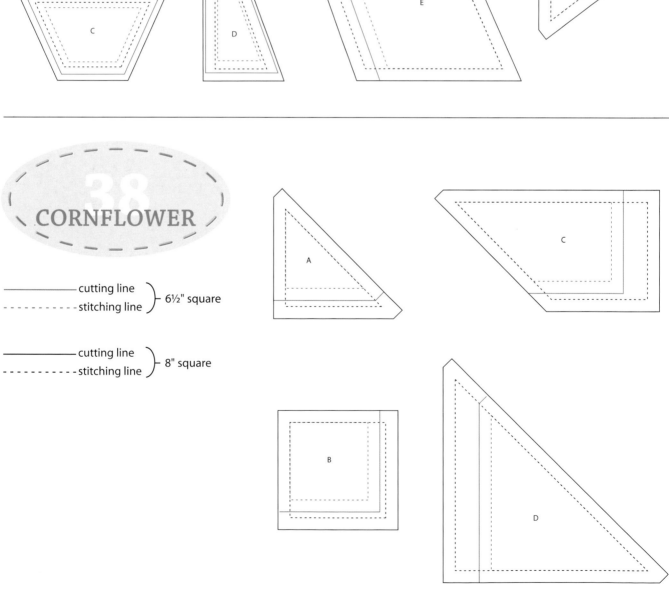

38 CORNFLOWER

⎯⎯⎯⎯ cutting line
- - - - - - - stitching line ⎬ 6½" square

⎯⎯⎯⎯ cutting line
- - - - - - - stitching line ⎬ 8" square

A

B

C

D

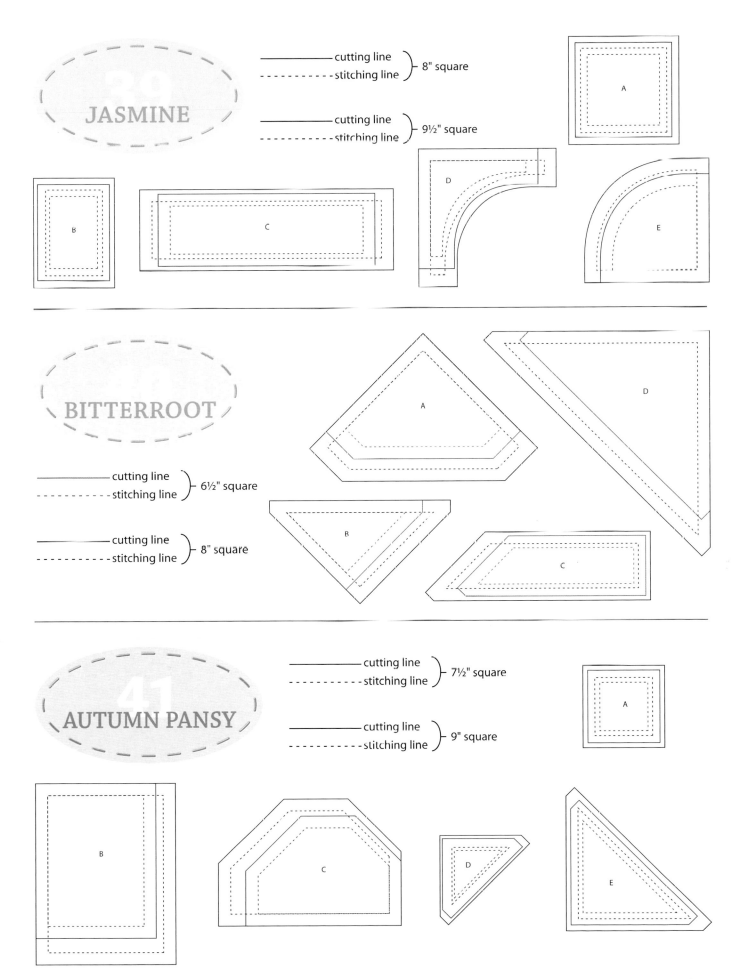

JASMINE

cutting line
stitching line ⟩ 8" square

cutting line
stitching line ⟩ 9½" square

A

B

C

D

E

BITTERROOT

cutting line
stitching line ⟩ 6½" square

cutting line
stitching line ⟩ 8" square

A

B

C

D

41 AUTUMN PANSY

cutting line
stitching line ⟩ 7½" square

cutting line
stitching line ⟩ 9" square

A

B

C

D

E

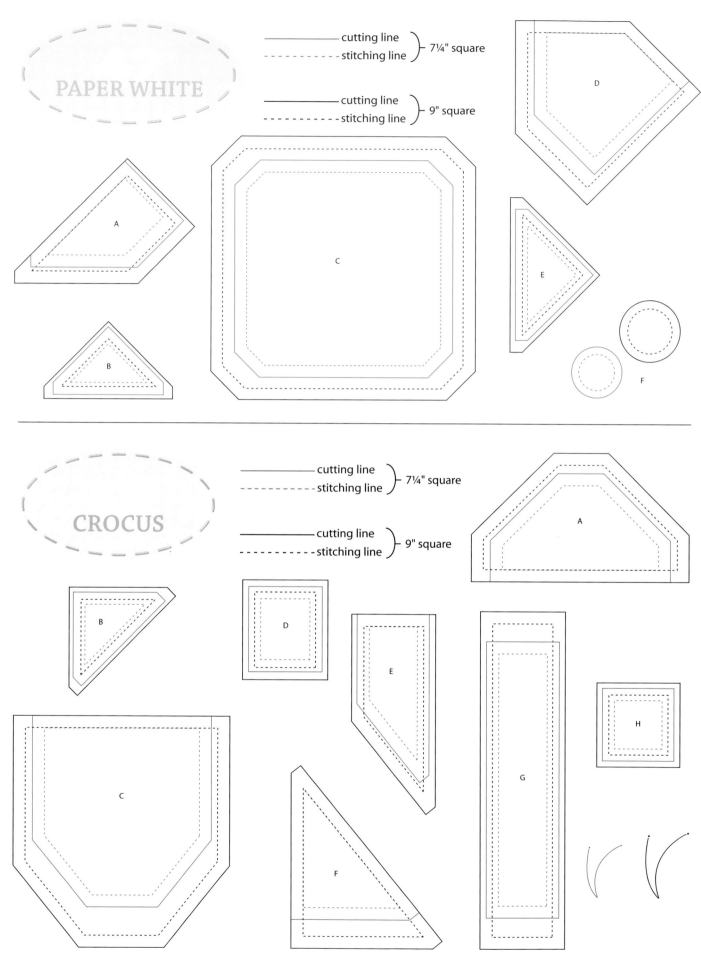

PAPER WHITE

cutting line
stitching line
} 7¼" square

cutting line
stitching line
} 9" square

A

B

C

D

E

F

CROCUS

cutting line
stitching line
} 7¼" square

cutting line
stitching line
} 9" square

A

B

C

D

E

F

G

H

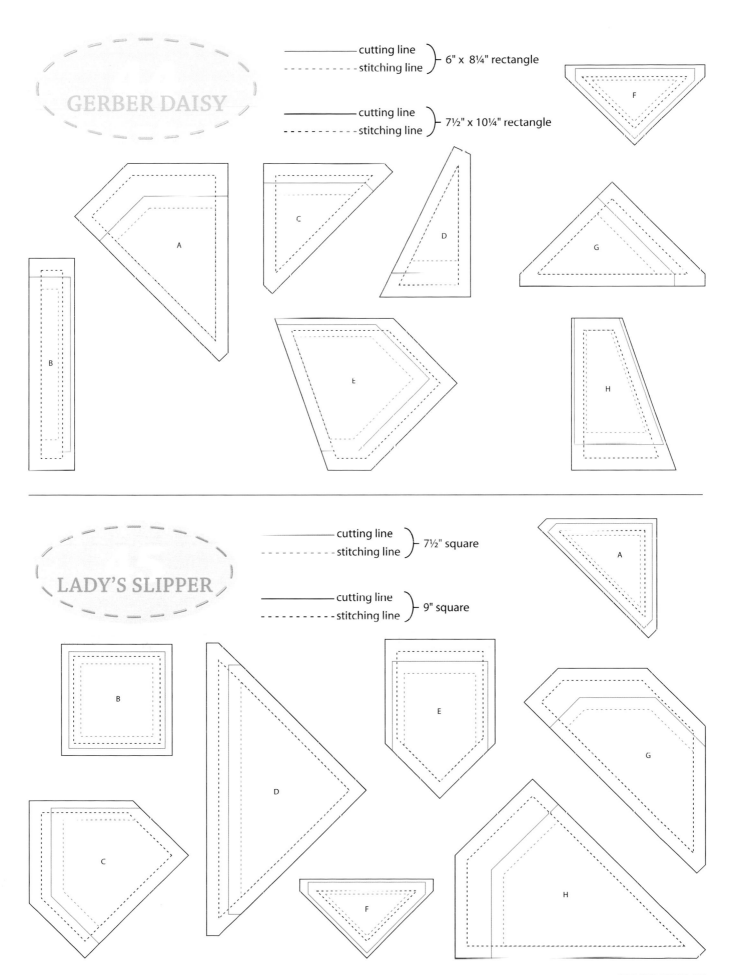

GERBER DAISY

cutting line
stitching line } 6" x 8¼" rectangle

cutting line
stitching line } 7½" x 10¼" rectangle

A

B

C

D

E

F

G

H

LADY'S SLIPPER

cutting line
stitching line } 7½" square

cutting line
stitching line } 9" square

A

B

C

D

E

F

G

H

Index

It's all on www.larkbooks.com

Got an idea for a book?
Read our book proposal guidelines and contact us.

Want to show off your work?
Browse current calls for entries.

Want to know what new and exciting books we're working on?
Sign up for our free e-newsletter.

Feeling crafty?
Find free, downloadable project directions on the site.

Interested in learning more about the authors, designers & editors who create Lark books?

Metric Conversion chart

INCHES	MILLIMETERS (MM)/ CENTIMETERS (CM)
1/8	3 mm
3/16	5 mm
1/4	6 mm
5/16	8 mm
3/8	9.5 mm
7/16	1.1 cm
1/2	1.3 cm
7/16	1.4 cm
5/8	1.6 cm
11/16	1.7 cm
3/4	1.9 cm
13/16	2.1 cm
7/8	2.2 cm
15/16	2.4 cm
1	2.5 cm
1 1/2	3.8 cm
2	5 cm
2 1/2	6.4 cm
3	7.6 cm
3 1/2	8.9 cm
4	10.2 cm
4 1/2	11.4 cm
5	12.7 cm
5 1/2	14 cm
6	15.2 cm
6 1/2	16.5 cm
7	17.8 cm
7 1/2	19 cm
8	20.3 cm
8 1/2	21.6 cm
9 (1/4 yard)	22.9 cm
9 1/2	24.1 cm
10	25.4 cm
10 1/2	26.7 cm
11	27.9 cm
11 1/2	29.2 cm
12	30.5 cm